MW01492361

Pentecostal Worship

GARY D. ERICKSON

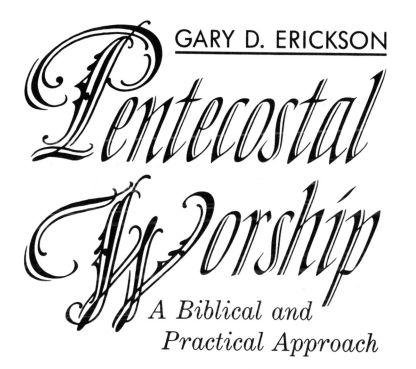

Pentecostal Worship

A Biblical and Practical Approach

Pentecostal Worship

Gary D. Erickson

©1989 Word Aflame Press
  Hazelwood, MO 63042-2299

Printing History: 1993, 1995, 1998

Cover Design by Tim Agnew

All Scripture quotations in this book are from the King James Version of the Bible unless otherwise identified.

All rights reserved. No portion of this publication may be reproduced, stored in an electronic system, or transmitted in any form or by any means, electronic, mechanical, photocopy, recording, or otherwise, without the prior permission of Word Aflame Press. Brief quotations may be used in literary reviews.

Printed in United States of America

WORD AFLAME®PRESS
8855 DUNN ROAD
HAZELWOOD, MO 63042-2299

Library of Congress Cataloging-in-Publication Data

Erickson, Gary D., 1948–
    Pentecostal worship : a Biblical and practical approach /
  by Gary D. Erickson.
        p. cm.
    Includes bibliographical references.
    ISBN 0-932581-52-8
    1. Public worship—Pentecostal churches. 2. Pentecostal churches-
  -Liturgy. I. Title.
  BX8762.Z5E75 1989
  264′.0994—dc20   89-38786
                                                             CIP

*To Mom and Dad
for the strong Christian influence
they have had on my life.*

Contents

Contents

Foreword

The hour cometh, and now is, when the true worshippers shall worship the Father in spirit and in truth (John 4:23).

The time *now is* for true worshipers to worship in spirit and in truth.

The essence of the first of the Ten Commandments was: Worship God and Him only (Exodus 20:3). Succinctly inserted in the last exhortation of Scripture is this command: "Worship God" (Revelation 22:9). The subject of worship is inexhaustible but *Pentecostal Worship* will contribute to a better understanding of this vital element of our relationship with God. Certainly, worship should be a free expression from the heart; however, it still must be controlled by divine authority. The ingredients for the incense of worship in the Tabernacle were precise as well as unique; God's instructions for acceptable worship are equally explicit.

Pentecostal Worship deals beautifully with important scriptural concepts regarding worship. Without a study on worship as God would have it, our worship can degenerate into a self-centered, self-oriented activity as we seek what blesses us rather than concentrating on our blessing Him. True worship consists of giving not getting, offering not receiving, blessing not being blessed!

The Bible repeatedly gives examples of acceptable and unacceptable worship, and these things "were written for our learning" (Romans 15:4). The harshest indictments in the Scriptures were directed at "unacceptable wor-

ship": from Cain to the "den of thieves" in the Temple.
The greatest commendations in the Scriptures were received because of acceptable worship: from Abel, Abraham, and David to the twenty-four elders casting their crowns before the throne saying, "Thou art worthy, O Lord, to receive glory and honour and power: for thou hast created all things, and for thy pleasure they are and were created" (Revelation 4:11).

Those who worship God must worship Him in spirit and in truth.

Worship "in spirit" alone is not enough. This fact was graphically illustrated when judgment fell in the midst of worship as David improperly transported the ark. In Jeremiah 6:19-20, God told the people, "Because [you] have not hearkened unto my words, nor to my law . . . your burnt offerings are not acceptable, nor your sacrifices sweet unto me."

Worship "in truth" alone is not enough. Of the people of God who had all the rituals and forms correct, God said, "This people honoureth me with their lips, but their heart is far from me. . . . In vain do they worship me" (Mark 7:6-7).

It is imperative that we learn what constitutes acceptable and unacceptable worship. Of the people who worshiped Him along with other gods of their own making, God said, "I hate, I despise your feast days, and I will not smell in your solemn assemblies" (Amos 5:21). Of the people who worshiped Him without obeying Him, He said, "When ye spread forth your hands, I will hide mine eyes from you: yea, when ye make many prayers, I will not hear" (Isaiah 1:15). Of the people who offered Him less than their best and felt their worship was a "weariness,"

He said, "Should I accept this of your hand? . . . Cursed be the deceiver, which . . . sacrificeth unto the Lord a corrupt thing" (Malachi 1:13-14).

Worship began before creation "when the morning stars sang together, and all the sons of God shouted for joy" (Job 38:7), and it will continue throughout eternity as we "worship him that liveth for ever and ever" (Revelation 4:10). Our purpose on earth is to worship! Our purpose in heaven will be to worship!

The author's objective in *Pentecostal Worship* is to help us become better worshipers, acceptable worshipers, true worshipers. "Ye also, as lively stones, are built up a spiritual house, an holy priesthood, to offer up spiritual sacrifices, acceptable to God by Jesus Christ" (I Peter 2:5). "The Father seeketh such to worship him" (John 4:23).

What more profitable study can we have than one on worship? I commend this book to you. Learn more about why . . . when . . . where . . . and how—and then WORSHIP! "He is thy Lord; and worship thou him" (Psalm 45:11).

The hour cometh, and now is, for *Pentecostal Worship*.

Anthony Mangun

Preface

This book is written to the *worship leader* as a resource of information and stimulus. It is written to the *worshiper* as a source of inspiration and exhortation. It is written to the *nonworshiper* as a beacon of enlightenment and allurement to embrace the essence of life's purpose. It is written to the *musician* as a strong cord of direction, as well as to inflame him or her with new zeal to give the maximum for the ultimate of purpose—worship.

Fresh winds are blowing in the world today. The fires of anointed worship are burning in more churches than ever. Thousands of new praise songs have been written, talent has been refined, new methods have been implemented, many books have been published, and a fresh enthusiasm has taken hold. Freedom in worship is even sweeping beyond denominational boundaries.

Solomon surely described this day when he wrote, "Of making many books there is no end" (Ecclesiastes 12:12). Why another book on worship? This book is unique in that it addresses the subject from a classical Pentecostal perspective. It is a practical manual, because it presents the basics of biblical worship. It will also serve as an inspirational tool. Chapter 8 is especially unique, for it deals with practical problems that are likely to arise in a worshiping church. For a church or an individual who is involved in worship, this book will also serve to fine-tune for greater purity and balanced treatment of this imperative ministry. Even many Pentecostals have developed traditions over the years, and it is hoped that this book will lead the reader to take a fresh look at what is biblical and what is not biblical about worship patterns today. This book is not a curious autopsy of some epoch of the past, but it is hoped that it will be the portrait of a healthy, worshiping church of today.

Once I began this project, I soon realized it was bigger than I was. The broadness of the subject is immeasurable and the depth is unfathomable. Nevertheless, I offer my thoughts on one of life's most important subjects, second only to salvation itself.

CHAPTER 1

·

The Restoration of Worship

When we look at what is happening in the world today, we see an effort to restore apostolic worship. The awakening of the church in the twentieth century is more than just another trend toward new techniques to achieve old goals. This revival of worship is directed toward a new goal: ministering to the Lord!

We have seen a renewed emphasis on holiness. Great strides have been made in the area of missions and evangelism. Accurate doctrine has brought about a great expansion of our understanding of God's Word. Human ingenuity has fostered a kaleidoscope of methods: bus ministry, discipleship programs, contests, church growth seminars, denominational programs, camp meetings, conferences, media programs, tent revivals, and specialized ministries, all of which have been a blessing. Nevertheless, a church without heart-felt worship is like a plastic replica of the real thing. Worship puts the emphasis on God's glory and not on human achievements. Worship is a spiritual catalyst that makes things happen!

The revival of true worship is overdue. Most churches in our world today are beehives of activity, yet the actual worship services are a bore. A. W. Tozer described the situation well: "In the average church the most real thing is the shadowy unreality of everything. The worshiper sits in a state of suspended meditation; a kind of dreamy numbness creeps upon him; he hears words but they do not register, he cannot relate them to anything on his own level."[1] When we compare many modern churches to the apostolic church of the first century we realize something is missing. When the first church came together things happened! "And when they had prayed, the place was shaken where they were assembled together; and they were all filled with the Holy Ghost, and they spake the word of God with boldness" (Acts 4:31).

The first church was unique in that many people in it had known Jesus personally. They had witnessed His ministry, death, and resurrection, and as a result their love for Him was fresh and keen. They were devoted first to their Lord and Savior who had risen from the dead and second to His teaching.

Although we cannot share with the first church in its unique position physically and historically, we can share with it spiritually. We can love Jesus with the same intensity and devotion as the first church. Worship transcends all ages, and it is a vital, life-producing ingredient in Christian service.

The apostolic church of the first century is a paradigm for Christian doctrine, conversion, methods of operation, ministry, and fellowship. Ephesians 2:20 says that we "are built upon the foundation of the apostles and prophets, Jesus Christ himself being the chief corner stone." Since the apostolic church is our pattern, it is very important for us to understand that it was a worshiping people. God desires that we worship just as the church that was born in Acts 2 did.

Our day has seen a great spiritual restoration. Much truth has been restored that was lost or obscured during the Dark Ages. We are seeing a revival of the baptism of the Holy Ghost evidenced by speaking in tongues, an experience that characterized the first church. There is also a revival of spiritual gifts, which the apostolic church enjoyed. Along with this restoration of truth and spiritual gifts is a restoration of apostolic worship.

There is a current interest in worship throughout Christendom. "We are living in a time when almost every major denomination has been affected by renewed interest in the history, theology, and practice of worship."[2] Many churches have been forced to evaluate their worship or lack of worship from a biblical perspective. There is a desire to turn from cold, formal traditions and return to real apostolic practices in worship. Even churches that have been practicing lively worship are wanting to fine-tune their efforts so as to add life to their services as never before.

All of this interest is not just happenstance. It is in the will of God.

David's Tabernacle

What is happening today is a restoration of the doctrine and practices of the New Testament church, and that church is a fulfillment of the prophecy of Amos: "In that day will I raise up the tabernacle of David that is fallen, and close up the breaches thereof; and I will raise up his

19

ruins, and I will build it as in the days of old" (Amos 9:11). Let us therefore consider the tabernacle of David.

The first tent revival in history was conducted by King David (I Chronicles 15-16). He located his tent on a hill called Mt. Zion on the southwest side of Jerusalem. The main attraction was the ark of the covenant, which was placed in the midst of this tabernacle. The activities around the tent may be compared to tent-revival services of today. There was singing, playing of musical instruments, and even shouting and dancing. The services were long and unrelenting. In fact, the Levites sang and worshiped every day, seven days a week. Their choirs and orchestras were arranged in shifts so there would be no break in their service of praise.

This was an extraordinary arrangement. The tabernacle of Moses was at Gibeon and the priests still offered their sacrifices there, without the ark of the covenant (I Chronicles 16:39; 21:29). Yet David's tabernacle became the center of praise and worship. God's approval was upon it, and it became a type of a greater day.

During the ministry of Eli the priest, the ark of God had been stolen by the Philistines. This caused great sorrow to Israel, for the ark of the covenant was a sacred object representing the presence of God. When Eli heard that the ark was stolen and that his sons were slain in battle, he fell backward, broke his neck, and died. His daughter-in-law also died upon hearing the news as she gave birth to a son. She named him Ichabod, meaning "the glory is departed." It was a dark day in Israel. (See I Samuel 4.)

Although the Philistines returned the ark to Israel after only seven months, the Israelites encountered many obstacles in bringing the ark to the location that God intended.

The Bethshemites of Israel were harvesting their wheat when two heifers sent by the Philistines pulled the ark, which was being carried on a cart, into their fields. They rejoiced to see it, but their rejoicing soon ended when people disrespectfully looked into the ark. As a result of this action, many people died. Frightened and bewildered, the people took the ark to the house of Abinadab in Kirjath-jearim and appointed his son Eleazar to keep it. It remained there for twenty years. (See I Samuel 6-7.)

During this time Saul was anointed king of Israel, and he led the nation downward spiritually and militarily. The Bible mentions the ark only once during Saul's reign (I Samuel 14:18). Saul was so out of touch with God that he did not perceive the supreme value of Israel's most sacred object. The silence concerning the ark during this period seems to reflect Israel's weak spiritual condition.

After Saul's death David became the king of Israel. After years of preparation, David had learned to trust the Lord and value His presence. He launched a campaign of reform that began with the return of the ark.

Even though his motives were pure, David's improper handling of the ark caused a serious problem. With thirty thousand men, he began a very lively procession carrying the ark to Jerusalem. A great orchestrated procession began a majestic journey from Abinadab's house with the ark mounted on a new cart. On the journey the oxen shook the ark. A man named Uzzah reached out to stabilize it and was smitten dead by God for his disobedience to the law. The procession stopped, and the people were confused and fearful. For three months the ark

21

remained at that place in the house of Obed-edom.

After searching the law David returned with the priests and Levites. This time they obeyed the Scriptures and carried the ark on the shoulders of the Levites.

So David went and brought the ark of God from the house of Obed-edom into the city of David with gladness. . . . And David danced before the LORD with all his might. . . . So David and all the house of Israel brought up the ark of the LORD with shouting, and with the sound of the trumpet. . . . And they brought in the ark of the LORD, and set it in his place, in the midst of the tabernacle that David had pitched for it (II Samuel 6:12-17).

No longer was the ark in obscurity, hidden away in a private home. The ark was brought into the city of Jerusalem, placed on Mt. Zion, and made the focal point of service unto the Lord. It was a refreshing symbol, for all to see, of Israel's returned glory.

David, being a musician, organized the first recorded musical program in the Bible. He took musical instruments and singing and made them tools of praise unto the Lord. It appears that before this time music in Israel was, for the most part, just extemporaneous expression without written music or words. The tabernacle of David became a place where the words of the prophets were sung with the accompaniment of musical instruments around the clock.

Asaph, Heman, and Jeduthun were appointed as music directors. They were given twenty-four choirs consisting of 288 choristers. Every choir with its leader consisted of twelve people. They served on a rotating schedule, offering praise to the Lord around the clock (I Chronicles 25). They were probably leaders for the 4,000 additional musicians mentioned in I Chronicles 23:5.

When the ark was placed in David's tabernacle, as recorded in I Chronicles 15-16, the singers lifted up their voices with joyful singing. The musicians played cymbals, harps, psalteries, trumpets, and cornets. The Israelites shouted for joy, and King David leaped and danced as the procession moved toward the ark's resting place. Their praise was demonstrative and exuberant, and the ark was the focal point of their enthusiasm. They had recovered the glory of God!

Let us visualize the scene. Gathered around a little tent perched on top of Mt. Zion were singing choirs and orchestras. Crowds of Hebrews congregated, many joining in the singing and praising. King David paid frequent visits to the tent to praise before the ark by lifting his hands, clapping his hands, shouting with a loud voice, bowing, dancing, and leaping. Perhaps David wrote many of the psalms in the very presence of the ark.

We can imagine King David kneeling before the ark under the tabernacle as he was anointed with a spirit of prophecy. The background was filled with music and singing. Recorders stood by to preserve his words. "I will sing of thy power; yea, I will sing aloud of thy mercy in the morning: for thou hast been my defense and refuge in the day of my trouble. Unto thee, O my strength, will I sing: for God is my defence, and the God of my mercy" (Psalm 59:16-17).

Mt. Sinai or Mt. Zion?

What significance does David's tabernacle have to modern times? Amos, the country prophet, prophesied that God would restore again the tabernacle of David. "In that day will I raise up the tabernacle of David that is fallen, and close up the breaches thereof; and I will raise up his ruins, and I will build it as in the days of old: that they may possess the remnant of Edom, and of all the heathen, which are called by my name, saith the LORD that doeth this" (Amos 9:11-12).

Acts 15 explains when and how this prophecy has been fulfilled. It records the first church council, which was called as a result of Judaizers insisting that Gentile converts be circumcised. Peter's experience at Cornelius's house in Acts 10 had already confirmed that Gentiles were permitted in the church. Now, some were teaching that they must become Jews by being circumcised. James, leader of the Jerusalem church, confirmed that the prophecy of Amos was being fulfilled at that moment (Acts 15:13-17). The doors of God's kingdom were flung open to all races and nationalities of people. Those who had experienced the new birth were to be embraced as full members of the body of Christ. The openness of David's tabernacle had been restored, not in a physical way, but in a spiritual fulfillment.

This fulfillment has many ramifications to the believer today, for we are an extension of that first church (Ephesians 2:20). The Day of Pentecost marked the beginning of this restoration (Acts 2).

The day on which God gave birth to the church is significant. The Feast of Pentecost was a Jewish harvest festival celebrated on the fiftieth day after the Feast of the Passover (Deuteronomy 16). The Jews later used it to commemorate the giving of the law at Mt. Sinai.

Mt. Sinai and Mt. Zion stand in contrast typologically, for Zion represents the church (Hebrews 12:22) and Sinai represents the Old Testament order. And according to tradition, the upper room in which the disciples met in Acts 1 was located on Mt. Zion. Thus both Mt. Sinai and Mt. Zion are commemorated on the same day: the Day of Pentecost! They represent the great dichotomy in God's dealings with man: the old covenant and the new covenant.

Sinai was cold law written on tables of stone. It was a mountain that was untouchable by the common people. It represents God's exposure of human sin and human inability to live up to God's standards. Sinai stands for rituals and formalities, for sacrifices of bulls and goats that foreshadowed God's plan of redemption. Contact with God was brief and only for a selected few.

The tabernacle of David was restored when Pentecost was moved from Sinai to Zion. Many spiritual types can be seen in this move. Let us consider briefly the significance of this restoration to the contemporary church.

1. Priesthood of all believers. David's tabernacle did not have a fence around it to prevent the common people from observing the activities. They, in a limited way, were even able to get involved. We are now a royal priesthood and a chosen generation (I Peter 2:9). We can come boldly into God's presence (Hebrews 4:16). Thus, at the death of Jesus, the veil in front of the ark in the Temple was torn from top to bottom, to signify that everyone could have free access to God through Christ (Matthew 27:51).

2. Salvation for all people. Amos said that "they may possess the remnant of Edom, and of all the heathen, which are called by my name" (Amos 9:12). Acts 2:39 confirms that this restoration includes all people: "to all that are afar off, even as many as the Lord our God shall call.'' (See also John 3:16.)

3. The introduction of a new order. David's tabernacle at Mt. Zion was a new thing. The old order continued at Gibeon without the ark. Today the Lord's presence no longer remains behind the veil. Now the Lord "tabernacles" within human lives (I Corinthians 6:19; II Corinthians 6:16).

4. A new dimension of worship. One of the most outstanding aspects of David's tabernacle was the praise and worship. Never had there been so much praise as in David's tabernacle. Worship had never involved so many people. It was never so artistic, intense, and relentless. Musical instruments had never been so generously used. The heartfelt participation was more that just another ritual.

It is this final meaning we want to explore further. David's God allowed a preview of better things to come. In the middle of the Old Testament God dropped this little refreshing interlude of spontaneity and exuberance. Sandwiched between rituals, priests, regimentation, and military conflicts, it stands out in stark contrast to much of the ceremony of the old order.

Apostolic Worship

The apostolic pattern forms a paradigm for the Christian belief system. The early church provides the model, and the Christian church today must be an extension of that original. It is from the apostles that we get our doctrine, structure, faith concepts, and godly lifestyle. Therefore, their methods and practice of worship are very important to the Christian church of today.

When we begin to look for clues to the way the early church worshiped, we find only limited information in Scripture. There are only hints, at best, as to the actual arrangement of church services and the methods employed. Although the New Testament is sparse in its historical description of worship, the Old Testament has an abundance of information. Instruction, commandments, and mechanics of operation are related in much detail in the Old Testament. This relative silence in the New Testament indicates that because of the indwelling Holy Spirit elaborate external guidelines are unnecessary. Our praise and worship should be spontaneous. Apostolic worship consists of voluntary heart-felt expression, not adherence to ceremony and ritual. (See John 7:38-39.)

Of course, worship in its broadest sense can incorporate many aspects of Christianity, such as preaching, teaching, fellowship, evangelism, and edification to the body. In our discussion, however, we want to focus on worship that is a direct ministry to the Lord.

There are several conclusions we can draw about apostolic worship from the Scriptures as well as the historical setting.

1. Since the early church was Jewish, to a great extent Old Testament patterns of worship were incorporated in apostolic worship.

"Christianity began among the Aramaic-speaking Jews and then spread to the Hellenistic Jewish community and eventually to the Gentiles."[3] The Aramaic Jews had strong ties to the Jewish tradition (Acts 21:20-21). In fact, the first church council was called because of Judaizers who were trying to make even Gentile Christians adhere to all of the Jewish law (Acts 15). They continued to frequent the Temple and synagogues (Acts 2:46; 13:5). They also continued to observe the Jewish hours of prayer (Acts 3:1).

Their worship practices took on a new meaning, however. Now, Jesus Christ was the center of everything! All believers became spiritual priests, with Jesus as the High Priest. God's true temple was no longer a building, but each believer became the temple of the Holy Ghost. They broke bread from house to house, eating with gladness and singleness of heart and praising God (Acts 2:46-47).

The Hellenistic Jews were influenced by Roman customs and were not as loyal to Jewish tradition. They spoke the Greek language, but they still were identified as Jews.

The Gentiles in the church had even less attachment to the law of Moses. Nevertheless, Jewish influence was still prevalent, for the Old Testament was their only written Bible at first and Jewish Christians were present even in Gentile cities. Paul's instructions to the Gentile church at Corinth give us some significant insights into the early church's worship methods.

2. Worship methods used in David's tabernacle were incorporated in the apostolic church.

First of all, the choirs, orchestras, and exuberant praise organized by David did not cease after his death. At the dedication of Solomon's Temple a vibrant worship service took place. The ark was brought from Mt. Zion and was placed in the new temple. At the dedication, the families of Asaph, Heman, and Jeduthun assembled to worship with music. "It came even to pass, as the trumpeters and singers were as one, to make one sound to be heard in praising and thanking the LORD; and when they lifted up their voice with the trumpets and cymbals and instruments of musick, and praised the LORD, saying, For he is good; for his mercy endureth for ever: that then the house was filled with a cloud, even the house of the LORD; so that the priests could not stand to minister by reason of the cloud: for the glory of the LORD had filled the house of God" (II Chronicles 5:13-14).

Solomon's Temple was destroyed by the Babylonians, and the Hebrews were held captive for seventy years. When they returned to restore the land, one of their first projects was to rebuild the Temple. When the foundation was complete they made the heavens ring with praise. The descendants of Asaph gathered trumpets and cymbals and praised the Lord with singing. Some people wept and others shouted aloud for joy until the noise was heard afar off (Ezra 3). After much difficulty, the Temple was completed. Again, it was the cause for great rejoicing.

As the restoration continued, Nehemiah inspired and supervised the rebuilding of the walls of Jerusalem. After struggling against great odds the walls were finally completed. Under the same leadership that David had appointed, Israel conducted a great celebration at the dedication of the wall. Nehemiah 12 describes this occasion of offering thanks to God. The Levites celebrated the dedication with thanksgiving, singing, cymbals, psalteries, and harps. They conducted a great procession upon the wall "with the musical instruments of David the man of God" (Nehemiah 12:36). "For in the days of David and Asaph of old there were chief of the singers, and songs of praise and thanksgiving unto God" (Nehemiah 12:46). "And [they] . . . rejoiced: for God had made them rejoice with

29

great joy: the wives also and the children rejoiced: so that the joy of Jerusalem was heard even afar off" (Nehemiah 12:43).

Although there is no single complete picture of worship in the New Testament, we find examples of group singing, loud group praying, expressions of great joy, and demonstrative behavior that onlookers compared to the actions of drunken men. It is reasonable to believe, as Robert Webber maintains, that the apostolic church continued to worship after the Old Testament patterns.[4] Since the praise featured at David's tabernacle became incorporated into the Jewish tradition, it is likely that the early church, which was Jewish, used similar modes of worship to express their intense spiritual experience. Chapter 6 will provide specific scriptural examples to show the similarity of physical expressions of worship in both testaments.

3. Apostolic worship is related to the tabernacle of David because it celebrated the resident presence of God within the believer.

David's tabernacle was erected to celebrate the recovery of the ark of the covenant by Israel. It focused importance upon the necessity of the presence of God. Apostolic worship celebrates that greatest miracle of the ages, "even the mystery which hath been hid from the ages and from generations, but now is made manifest to his saints: . . . which is Christ in you, the hope of glory" (Colossians 1:26-27).

There is a story about a missionary who was working in China. He gave a Bible to an old Chinese man and asked him to find the greatest miracle in this book of miracles. The missionary left and returned several months later. He asked the old man to tell him what he had found. The old Chinese man said, "The greatest miracle in this book was easy to find. This miracle exceeds all others. I am filled with wonder that the great God of heaven would come and live in this old Chinese man's heart!" Apostolic worship is predicated upon the wonderful indwelling of the Holy Ghost.

David's tabernacle is restored in us. We have become the tabernacle. God now resides within the heart of every person who has been born again (Galatians 2:20; Ephesians 3:17-18; I John 3:24). This wonderful experience stimulates worship. When the Jews at Pentecost were baptized with the Holy Ghost, they were accused of being drunk (Acts 2:13). The joy of the Lord was so real that they appeared to be inebriated on wine.

Ephesians 5:19-20 describes one of the results of the Spirit's indwelling: "Speaking to yourselves in psalms and hymns and spiritual songs, singing and making melody in your heart to the Lord: giving thanks always for all things." Colossians 3:16 similarly instructs: "Let the word of Christ dwell in you richly in all wisdom; teaching and admonishing one another in psalms and hymns and spiritual songs, singing with grace in your hearts to the Lord."

As David's tabernacle celebrated the presence of the ark in the midst of Israel, so apostolic worship celebrates the presence of God within the believer. And God's abiding presence causes worship to emanate forth with spontaneity.

Although the New Testament is not as explicit as the Old in describing methods of worship, it is clear that Jesus Christ became the focal point of worship; the Old Testa-

ment institutions of worship were fulfilled in Him. There
is no indication that worship diminished in intensity. If
any change was made, it resulted in an increase in the
depth and feeling of the worship experience.

Contemporary Fulfillment

Since the turn of the century, there has been an extraordinary outpouring of the Spirit of God. Many denominational churches have experienced outbreaks of the baptism of the Holy Ghost among their membership. Many
people are seeking to return to the apostolic church pattern for doctrine, gifts, and miracles. Along with this
restoration, there is a renewed interest in worship, praise,
and thanksgiving.

Many churches have taken a new look at their worship practices in an effort to achieve a fresher, more meaningful expression. Dead, ritualistic patterns that do not
lift the heart have been abandoned for lively methods that
allow participation by the believer.

There have been many innovations in the area of
music. Words of songs have become more scriptural and
worshipful. Many of the larger churches have a director
or minister of music whose chief responsibility is to lead
the church into a worship experience.

The trends we are seeing are a fulfillment of the
restoration spoken of by Joel. Peter confirmed that Joel's
prophecy was fulfilled at Pentecost (Acts 2:16), yet complete fulfillment is still being realized in the kingdom of
God. Joel spoke of a former rain and a latter rain of God's
mighty outpouring: "For he hath given you the former
rain moderately, and he will cause to come down for you
the rain, the former rain, and the latter rain in the first

month" (Joel 2:23). The first outpouring was called moderate, indicating that the latter-day outpouring will be greater than the former. And it is exciting to realize that we are living in the time of the latter rain.

As a part of the great restoration spoken of by Joel, God is leading people into a renewal of scriptural worship.

Notes

[1] A. W. Tozer, *The Divine Conquest* (Harrisburg, PA: Christian Publishers, 1950), p. 90.

[2] Robert E. Webber, *Worship Is a Verb,* (Grand Rapids, MI: Zondervan Publishing House, 1982), p. 11.

[3] Ibid., p. 37.

[4] Ibid., p. 43.

C H A P T E R 2

Thanksgiving, Praise, and Worship

he only time anyone shouts in some churches is at the business meeting. The church service is kept low-keyed deliberately so as to maintain a "reverent" posture. There is no joy in the singing, the prayers are petrified deadness, and the sermons are a cure for insomnia.

A church that does not promote a thankful attitude and that does not encourage the believers to offer the sacrifice of praise will never experience the joy of real worship. The religion of its members will consist of an endurance contest to do their duty.

While doing visitation work, my wife and I met a family that expressed to us their exasperation with formal churches. Apparently, they had visited a number of churches in our area and were not satisfied with any of them. We convinced them that our church was different, and they promised to attend.

We were nervous that Sunday morning, knowing our visitors were there to critique. As the service progressed, the singing was loud and full. The hand clapping accented the peppy rhythm. When hands were raised in praise and shouts of joy rang out across the sanctuary, we knew our visitors were going to experience their first exposure to apostolic worship.

At the close of the service we were eager to learn their opinion of what they experienced. We were relieved when the mother expressed her feeling by saying, "This is the first time in my life I have ever gone to church and had fun!" Her statement may sound odd, but does church have to be a bore?

Many people know God in a limited way but do not really enjoy Him. This is not God's intention. One of the chief purposes for our existence is to worship God. The twenty-four elders in Revelation 4:11 said, "Thou art worthy, O Lord, to receive glory and honour and power: for thou hast created all things, and for thy pleasure they are and were created." Thanksgiving, praise, and worship are ministries to the Lord that lift us into an experience with God that is enjoyable for both us and Him. God receives His greatest pleasure when we worship Him. According to Jesus' words in John 4:23, the Father seeks worshipers.

In this chapter we will define three terms—*thanksgiving, praise,* and *worship*—and use them to explain our progressive approach toward God in this important and special ministry. When we attempt to express the mysteries of God, words sometimes become clumsy tools. Worship is one of those almost inexplicable areas of God's mysteries. While this discussion will not be perfect, perhaps it will contribute to a better understanding of this wonderful and imperative element of our relationship with God. These three definitions are not given in order to draw lines and compartmentalize our devotional experience. It is impossible to pigeonhole something so sacred and ethereal as worship with terms and labels. Becoming too analytical will hinder rather than help. We can experience the joy of worship without bothering to consciously cross these boundaries of terminology as we ascend in ministry unto the Lord.

Thanksgiving

Thanksgiving is an attitude of *gratefulness for what God has done*. It is a prevailing mental state of thankfulness toward God. Praise and worship become impossible without this predominant feeling of gratitude. Thanksgiving is the first step toward worship; thanksgiving gets us moving in the right direction.

Thanksgiving requires a probing of our memory to recall personal blessings. It means acknowledging the Lord as the source of all good things. Instead of simply consuming God's blessings, we celebrate His abundant provisions.

Unthankfulness is the root cause of many sins of the flesh and spirit. According to Romans 1, unthankfulness produces great spiritual problems for those who know God but do not acknowledge Him. Romans 1:21 says, "Because that, when they knew God, they glorified him not as God, neither were thankful; but became vain in their imaginations, and their foolish heart was darkened." This verse and the verses that follow it indicate that unthankfulness is not just another problem but rather the source of problems. It is staggering to consider the horrible results of an unthankful attitude as listed in Romans 1. The unthankful people described there

1. Became vain in their imaginations.

2. Caused their heart to be darkened.

3. Became fools.

4. Changed the glory of God into images of man, birds, beasts, and creeping things.

5. Became unclean through lust to dishonor their bodies between themselves.

6. Changed truth into a lie.

7. Worshiped and served the creature more than the Creator.

8. Became vile in their affections, men and women engaging in homosexuality.

9. Received a reprobate mind.

10. Became filled with unrighteousness, fornication, wickedness, covetousness, maliciousness, envy, murder, debate, deceit, malignity, and became whisperers, backbiters, haters of God, despiteful, boasters, inventors of evil, disobedient to parents, lacking in understanding, covenant breakers, without natural affection, implacable, unmerciful.

11. Became worthy of death.

Many problems of our nation and the world are the direct result of unthankfulness. The Bible predicts that unthankfulness will be rampant in the last days (II Timothy 3:1-2). And indeed, we are seeing this sickness prevail, for the more people get the more they want, and they do not take time to be grateful. Once their wants are gratified without delay, they move on restlessly with more wants. Mark Twain once said, "If you pick up a starving dog and make him prosperous, he will not bite you. This is the principal difference between a dog and a man."[1]

Jesus expressed great displeasure toward those with an unthankful attitude. After pronouncing ten lepers healed, He sent them to the priest to be declared legally cured. As they went they were healed. Yet only one returned to offer thanksgiving, prompting Jesus to ask, "Where are the nine?" (Luke 17:17). Being thankful requires that we push aside current problems and needs and focus on past and present blessings. We must activate our memory, which requires energy and concentration.

Perhaps one purpose of the many memorials God has instituted throughout history is to motivate thankfulness. For the Hebrews, He ordained feasts, offerings, and memorials. The ark of the covenant contained a bowl of manna to remind them of God's provision. It contained Aaron's rod that budded to remind them of the greatness of God's power. The Ten Commandments on the tables of stone were also inside the ark to remind Israel of God's eternal law. (See Exodus 16:33-34; Numbers 17:10; Deuteronomy 10:5; Hebrews 9:4.)

When the Israelites crossed the Jordan River, the Lord instructed them to build a memorial on the bank with twelve stones from the river. Future generations would see this pile of stones and ask, "What mean ye by these stones?" (Joshua 4:6). This question would give the people an opportunity to tell the story again of their miraculous crossing. Thus the memorial was an aid to generate a perpetual thankfulness among God's people.

In the Book of Deuteronomy, which is a book of remembrance, Moses warned Israel not to forget. When they were enjoying the abundance of the land, he said, "Then beware lest thou forget the LORD, which brought thee forth out of the land of Egypt" (Deuteronomy 6:12). God knew that forgetfulness would lead to unthankfulness.

At the Last Supper with His disciples, Jesus instituted a memorial with the fruit of the vine and the broken bread (Matthew 26:26-29). When we partake of the Eucharist, it reminds us of the great sacrifice Jesus made when His blood was shed and His body was broken. Here again a memorial reminds us to be thankful.

Before we can move toward God in the ministry of praise and worship, thanksgiving must be our first step. Thanksgiving takes us to the bright side of life. It germinates a positive attitude toward God that can begin growing into a lively relationship of praise and worship. It is impossible to enter into praise if we do not have an attitude of gratitude toward God.

Being thankful is an humbling experience because it makes us subject to someone outside ourselves. It causes us to acknowledge that we need someone else to contribute to our happiness. It is humbling to the ego, which wants to be self-sufficient. A proud person will have difficulty being thankful.

Thankfulness also requires selflessness. A selfish person is usually an unthankful person. Giving thanks is outside the realm of our own needs. It reaches into the life of others and requires a giving of ourselves.

Being thankful also involves a sacrifice. It is not a natural virtue of fallen humanity. If we follow our carnal nature we will have an unthankful state of mind. To be thankful we must go against our basic nature, which is preoccupied with wants instead of blessings.

It is disturbing to see Christian ministries that focus on blessings and provisions to the point of an imbalance. Principles of discipleship and consecration are equally important. As John MacArthur wrote, "Today in much of contemporary Christianity, Jesus is seen as a genie who responds to our wishes. After receiving our wishes, we often abandon any meaningful relationship with him. Jesus is offered as a panacea for one's ills, and little else. We are guilty of ingratitude toward Christ."[2]

This attitude drives people in pursuit of selfish and materialistic wants. But after a person fulfills them he finds that happiness is gone, and his attention is attracted to more wants. We must break this vicious cycle by learning to curb our wants so that we can obey the admonition of the apostle Paul: "In every thing give thanks: for this is the will of God in Christ Jesus concerning you" (I Thessalonians 5:18).

If someone has difficulty in really being able to praise the Lord it could be that he is not genuinely grateful. Perhaps some disappointment or severe trial of life has left him a little embittered. But we cannot move any farther in praise and worship until we are thankful.

Praise

Praise and thanksgiving are closely joined together. As we have already stated, thanksgiving acknowledges what God has done. Praise *acknowledges who God is*. We do not want to be overly analytical with definitions to the point of becoming mechanical, yet pointing out a distinction in these areas of fellowship with God can direct us toward a richer and a more expanded ministry to the Lord.

Praise is not just a feeling or an attitude; it is an expression. Praise includes verbally extolling the virtues and divine attributes of God. It also includes physical, bodily expression such as hand clapping, raising of the hands, leaping, playing a musical instrument, or even dancing. These are all scriptural ways of praising the Lord. (See chapter 6.)

Praise means esteeming God's greatness and venerating His holy character. It is confessing Him by all His glorious titles and virtues with heart-felt meaning. Praise is agreeing with all the things God has said about Himself in His Word. As we begin to understand the infinite grandeur of the Almighty, we will praise Him spontaneously. In praise we become poised for a deeper experience—worship.

Since praise is an expression, praising God does not mean being silent and still. Praise is expressing outwardly a feeling or an understanding of admiration for the Lord. This expression will be verbal, audible, or demonstrative.

Praise can be given *verbally* through speaking and singing.

• *And my tongue shall speak of thy righteousness and of thy praise all the day long* (Psalm 35:28).

• *And he hath put a new song in my mouth, even praise unto our God* (Psalm 40:3).

• *I will sing of the mercies of the LORD for ever: with my mouth will I make known thy faithfulness to all generations* (Psalm 89:1).

• *Accept, I beseech thee, the freewill offerings of my*

mouth, O LORD, and teach me thy judgments (Psalm 119:108).

• *My lips shall utter praise* (Psalm 119:171).

• *Cry out and shout, thou inhabitant of Zion: for great is the Holy One of Israel in the midst of thee* (Isaiah 12:6).

• *Therefore let us offer the sacrifice of praise to God continually, that is, the fruit of our lips giving thanks to his name* (Hebrews 13:15).

• *And after these things I heard a great voice of much people in heaven, saying, Alleluia; Salvation, and glory, and honour, and power, unto the Lord our God* (Revelation 19:1).

Praise can be offered by percussive and melodic instruments of music. The emphasis here is on *audible* praise.

• *Praise the LORD with harp: sing unto him with the psaltery and an instrument of ten strings* (Psalm 33:2).

• *O clap your hands, all ye people; shout unto God with the voice of triumph* (Psalm 47:1).

• *Praise him with the sound of the trumpet: praise him with the psaltery and harp. Praise him with the timbrel and dance: praise him with stringed instruments and organs. Praise him upon the loud cymbals: praise him upon the high sounding cymbals* (Psalm 150:3-5).

• *And Miriam . . . took a timbrel in her hand; and all the women went out after her with timbrels and with dances* (Exodus 15:20).

• *It came even to pass, as the trumpeters and singers were as one, to make one sound to be heard in praising and thanking the LORD; and when they lifted up their voice with the trumpets and cymbals and instruments of musick, and praised the LORD . . .* (II Chronicles 5:13).

Praise can also be *demonstrative.*

• *Thus will I bless thee while I live: I will lift up my hands in thy name* (Psalm 63:4).

• *Lift up your hands in the sanctuary, and bless the LORD* (Psalm 134:2).

• *And he leaping up stood, and walked, and entered with them into the temple, walking, and leaping, and praising God* (Acts 3:8).

• *Let them praise his name in the dance* (Psalm 149:3).

• *And David danced before the LORD with all his might* (II Samuel 6:14).

Praise is a biblical word. The word *praise* occurs over two hundred times in the English Bible. As many as a dozen different Hebrew and Greek words are used to convey the idea of praise. Thus praise can have various shades of meaning, depending on the context and original word used.

Dr. Robert D. Bergen, a linguist, has compiled an interesting study on the word *praise* from the Hebrew and the Greek. This study is found in Jack Taylor's book, *The Hallelujah Factor.*[3] It is interesting to discover that many Greek and Hebrew words in the original text are associated with praise, although some are not translated in our Bible as "praise"—fifty in Hebrew and twenty-six in Greek. We will list some of these words as they relate to the three areas of praise we have considered.

Hebrew[4]

1. Words meaning vocalized praise

English Transliteration	Meaning	Times Used
hallal	laud, boast, celebrate	99
gil	shout, circle in joy	29
tehillah	sing hallals	50
saphar	recount, proclaim	18
shabach	shout	7
ranan	shout with joy	42

2. Words meaning audible praise

English Transliteration	Meaning	Times Used
zamar	pluck strings of an instrument	40
maha	clap	1
neginah	music, song, string	8
nagan	play string instrument	2

3. Words meaning demonstrative praise

English Transliteration	Meaning	Times Used
yadah	worship with extended hands	90
barak	kneel, bless, salute	70
todah	extend the hands in praise	32
ragad	dance, skip about	1

| sahag | play, dance | 4 |
| pazaz | leap | 1 |

Greek[5]

1. Words meaning vocalized praise

English Transliteration	Meaning	Times Used
ainesis, ainos, aineo	laud, boast, celebrate	14
epainos, epaineo	strengthened form of ainos	17
exomologeomai	confess forth openly, freely	11
humneo, humnos	to sing praises	6

2. Words meaning audible praise

English Transliteration	Meaning	Times Used
psallo	twitch, twang, play musical instrument	12

3. Words meaning demonstrative praise

English Transliteration	Meaning	Times Used
eulogatos, eulogia	kneel, bless, salute	21
allomai	leap	1
gonupeteo	kneel down	4
kampto	to bend the knee	2
pipto	to fall to the ground	15
proskuneo	to fall down and worship	42
skirtao	to leap with joy	3

This list of Greek and Hebrew words associated with praise is not complete, but it is a sampling that illustrates the nature of praise from a biblical perspective.

Praise is not just pondering God's glorious nature and works, but praise is an offering of expressed gratitude and appreciation. It is an exhibit of love and adoration displayed before the Lord as proof of our faith in Him. Praise is the voice of faith, confirming His glory and omnipotence.

Praise is often a spontaneous, heart-felt expression. The psalmist said, "May my lips overflow with praises" (Psalm 119:171, NIV). Sometimes praise is an overflow of inward joy. It comes forth unforced, almost as an involuntary response of joy before the Lord. But sometimes it is an offering of sacrifice, a crucifixion of the flesh, a forcing of our lips and vocal cords to conform to the will of the Spirit. Hebrews 13:15 speaks of offering "the sacrifice of praise to God continually, that is, the fruit of our lips giving thanks to his name." Other passages of Scripture also mention the sacrifice of thanksgiving or praise, indicating a deliberate, planned expression (Psalm 107:22; 116:17; Jeremiah 17:26; 33:11).

Habakkuk recorded for us his dialogue with God concerning the disparity of justice. After he complained to God about the iniquities around him, God revealed to him that the just shall live by faith (Habakkuk 2:4). Habakkuk therefore concluded, "Although the fig tree shall not blossom, neither shall fruit be in the vine; the labour of the olive shall fail, and the fields shall yield no meat; the flock shall be cut off from the fold, and there shall be no herd in the stalls: yet I will rejoice in the LORD, I will joy in the God of my salvation" (Habakkuk 3:17-18).

Praise can be offered regardless of circumstances. It may not always be an emotional response; sometimes it will simply originate in a deliberate decision of the will. It is the will of God that we praise Him at all times. The psalmist said, "Seven times a day do I praise thee" (Psalm 119:164). "I will bless the LORD at all times: his praise shall continually be in my mouth" (Psalm 34:1).

Worship

In a general sense, worship can encompass all positive interaction and communication between creation and the Creator, including thanksgiving and praise, but for the purposes of our study let us focus on worship as the ultimate dimension in our interaction with the Almighty God. Thanksgiving lays the foundation of a good attitude. Praise carries us into the next phase of progression by giving expression to our adoration of God. But worship is the apex of communion with God. It is a supernatural, mutual exchange between humanity and deity, anointed with the Spirit and permeated with love.

The English word *worship* is a very good word to describe this ministry unto the Lord. It comes from the Anglo-Saxon word *weorthscipe,* which was modified to *worthship* and then to *worship.* The root meaning of *worship,* then, is "to attribute worth" to something or someone.[6] Worship is comprehending and acknowledging the worth-ship of the Lord Jesus Christ. Although our finite minds cannot completely understand His greatness, we can become cognizant of a measure of His immense splendor. Even a limited understanding of God's majesty is enough to invoke awe and wonder.

Worship is entering the throne room of the King of

kings. This privilege should excite a desire in us to visit the Lord in worship frequently. Certain preparation should be made before making our entrance into His majestic presence. Even though Hebrews 4:16 tells us to "come boldly unto the throne of grace," it does not mean to do so disrespectfully. In fact, Zondervan's interlinear New Testament renders "boldly" as "with confidence."[7] When we come into His throne room we should come with confidence that He will be faithful. But we should not come empty handed. We should not barge into His presence rudely, without proper respect. We are His children, and a king will permit certain privileges to His children, but as mature children we should learn to enter His courts with praise and thanksgiving (Psalm 100:4). When the disciples asked the Lord to teach them to pray, He began His model prayer with these words: "Our Father which art in heaven, Hallowed be thy name" (Matthew 6:9). If Jesus approached God in praise, so should we.

Queen Esther, even though she was the queen, made preparation before she entered the king's chamber. In her case it was more than etiquette. By her statement "If I perish, I perish" we know it could have cost her life to go before the king uninvited (Esther 4:16). She fasted and had her people fast. She also put on her royal apparel so she might look her best. We should go before our King in humility and put on the "garment of praise" (Isaiah 61:3).

Before the priest could enter the Tabernacle to minister, certain preparations were necessary at the brazen altar and the laver of water. So should we prepare before entering into God's presence with the "calves of our lips" (Hosea 14:2). Offering the sacrifice of praise

49

prepares us to enter His presence in worship.

In the original languages of the Old and New Testaments, worship means to bow down in obeisance. The worship of God is not explicitly defined in the Scripture, but it seems to mean a more serious adoration of praise. Vine explained, "Broadly it may be regarded as the direct acknowledgment to God of His nature, attributes, ways and claims, whether by the outgoing of the heart in praise and thanksgiving or deed done in such acknowledgment."[8] Worship, in the broader sense, encompasses many aspects of Christian activity. But in this study we will examine worship as a direct ministry unto the Lord.

To explain what we mean by direct ministry unto the Lord, perhaps the illustration below will be helpful.

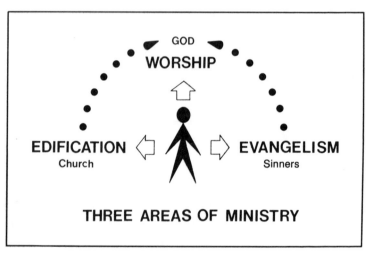

Fig. 1

Ministering to others outside our own needs can be divided into three areas: evangelism, edification, and worship.

Evangelism is reaching out to the lost by verbal witnessing, interceding in prayer, living a good Christian life before them, and showing helpful kindness. Reaching out to the world with love and concern is the ministry of evangelism.

Edification is a ministry to our own brothers and sisters in the Lord by showing love and kindness, teaching, interceding in prayer for one another, setting an example in faithfulness, being used in the gifts of the Spirit, and any other edifying acts directed toward the church. (See John 13:35; I Corinthians 14:1-4.)

Evangelism and edification are indirect ministries. They are done unto the Lord, but in an indirect way. The Lord said, "Inasmuch as ye have done it unto one of the least of these my brethren, ye have done it unto me" (Matthew 25:40). Ministering to others can be called a horizontal ministry. We are ministering unto the Lord, but indirectly through others.

Worship is different. No one else is necessary, because it is an exchange between the individual and God alone. Thus, worship is a direct ministry. It is a mutual love relationship of holy communion.

It is possible to be very busy working for the Lord in the horizontal area while neglecting the important ministry of worship. Of course, our goal should be to strike a balance in all these areas of ministry.

The incense offered upon the altar of incense in the Tabernacle is a beautiful type of prayer and worship (Psalm 141:2; Revelation 8:3). A special mixture of spices was allowed to smolder on a bed of coals taken from the brazen altar twice each day. A sweet aroma would fill the Tabernacle and then drift into the courtyard and into the camp of Israel. The pleasant smell was a comfort to the people that everything was all right in the Tabernacle.

The apothecaries were given a special recipe for the incense. They blended together four sweet spices: stacte, onycha, galbanum, and frankincense (Exodus 30:34-38). One-half of the mixture was composed of the first three elements and half the mixture was frankincense. The Hebrews were forbidden to duplicate this compound for their personal use, for it was only to be a sweet savor, holy unto the Lord. If the incense was made properly, the Lord promised to meet the priest at the altar (Exodus 30:36).

The first half of the mixture can be compared to our efforts toward God in worship, while the other half seems to represent God's participation. Each of the first three spices—stacte, onycha, and galbanum—have interesting characteristics that can be instructive for our worship.

Stacte was an aromatic gum or resin produced by a desert shrub. This substance would ooze forth from the plant in drops. The Hebrew word for stacte means "a drop" due to its flowing out in drops.[9] The plant seemed to yield its sweet resin freely. So should we offer worship spontaneously. Our adoration should exude from a sincere heart. If "worship" is forced, it is not a sweet savor unto the Lord. No one can force us to worship; real worship is a voluntary act.

During David's festival of praise at the return of the ark to Jerusalem, the people were lifted into true, spontaneous worship. Their sincerity and passion is evident as their praises reached a zenith: "Let the heavens be glad, and let the earth rejoice: and let men say among the nations, The LORD reigneth. Let the sea roar, and the fulness thereof: let the fields rejoice, and all that is therein" (I Chronicles 16:31-32).

Onycha was taken from a crustaceous animal of the deep. *Wilson's Old Testament Word Studies* suggests that it came from the shell of a species of mussel found in the lakes of India.[10] When crushed and burned, it emitted a musky odor. Likewise, our worship should issue forth from a deep, heart-felt commitment. The deepest part of the human nature is the spirit. When we worship from the spirit we go beyond intellect and emotions and enter into communion with God. Worship is a coming together of God's Spirit and the human spirit in the highest communion of mutual love. The psalmist expressed this depth of relationship: "Deep calleth unto deep at the noise of thy waterspouts: all thy waves and thy billows are gone over me" (Psalm 42:7).

Galbanum was a resin taken from a plant of the parsley family. Alone, galbanum had an unpleasant smell, but when mixed in the proper proportion with the other spices it contributed to the potency and the exhilarating effect of the aroma.[11] Worship likewise is an intense experience, powerful and exhilarating! It is impossible to worship passively. The twenty-four elders in Revelation 4 cast their crowns before God, saying, "Thou art worthy, O Lord, to receive glory and honour and power: for thou hast created all things, and for thy pleasure they are and were created" (Revelation 4:11). In our worship we extol God's glory, honor, and power. Compared to God's worthiness our efforts are inadequate. Therefore, we should worship with all the intensity we can muster. "Let the high praises of God be in their mouth" (Psalm 149:6).

The second half of the incense mixture can be seen as representing God's part in worship. Just as the Lord promised Israel that He would meet them at the altar of incense, so has He promised to meet us in worship (Psalm 22:3). In worship, God becomes a participator.

Frankincense formed one-half of the aromatic mixture. It came from a scrubby tree in the Middle East. Scraping the bark of the tree caused the gum to ooze forth from the limbs. After it dried, it was collected by gatherers and crushed. When crushed it turned white, the color of purity. It was also very expensive. The wise men valued it highly by offering it with gold and myrrh as a gift to the Christ Child (Matthew 2:11). Similarly, to us the Lord is like a precious commodity, the "pearl of great price," "treasure hid in a field."

We should offer thanksgiving and praise until they are blended with that heavenly ingredient we call anointing. Our approach to the throne room of God should be paved with stepping stones of thanksgiving and praise. Entering into His presence is an exhilarating experience of mutual interaction. We bless Him, and He blesses us! As we offer to Him our incense of adoration and devotion, He imparts to us strength from His Spirit.

Worship, in this context, is more than a thrill of excitement that produces a party-like atmosphere. It is more than a tingle and a shiver of sensation. Worship is standing in the throne room of God! A solemnity grips us in His presence. The awesomeness of the Almighty demands our reverence. His omnipotence compels our obeisance. The presence of the King of kings reveals sin, evokes commitment, and examines every fiber of the soul.

When Isaiah was carried by the Spirit into the throne room of God, he cried out, "Woe is me! for I am undone; because 1 am a man of unclean lips, and I dwell in the midst of a people of unclean lips: for mine eyes have seen the King, the LORD of hosts" (Isaiah 6:5). He did not leap, dance, or shout, but he bowed in reverence and respect. He was keenly aware of his unworthiness and was humbled in the presence of God.

God is the epitome of holiness, purity, and righteousness. He is infinite in strength. His wisdom is likewise infinite. God is totally independent and self-sufficient. When we stand in the presence of such excellence our fleshly limitations are revealed. Our fallen state and our inferior position are a sharp contrast to His matchless presence.

We frequently enjoy services in which praises are offered to God in a variety of expressions. It is a joyous experience to see uninhibited people expressing their praise. But we also need services in which everyone falls on his knees in humble adoration, a holy reverence envelops the congregation, and people cry out in humble self-abasement and lay prostrate in God's presence. Could it be that we sometimes stop short of giving ourselves totally in worship? We must never forget that the purpose of worship is not just to edify ourselves, but it is also to give ourselves to the Lord that He might have pleasure in us.

The original languages of the Bible reveal that worship is a deep adoration of God. Let us notice the humility illustrated in these word meanings.[12]

Hebrew

English Transliteration	Meaning	Times Used
yadah	worship with extended hands	90
barak	kneel, bless, salute	70
harah	worship, kneel, prostrate	65

Greek

English Transliteration	Meaning	Times Used
eulogatos, eulogia	corresponds with barak	21
psallo, psalmos	sing praises in spiritual ecstasy	4
gonupeteo	kneel down	4
kampto	bend the knee	2
pipto	fall to the ground	15
proskuneo	fall down and worship	42
hosanna	"Save, Lord"	5

The Bible is full of examples of bowing, kneeling, and showing humble adoration. (See chapter 6.)

To summarize the meaning of worship in the context of a direct ministry unto the Lord, let us consider the following points.

1. Worship is more than an attitude or an expression. It is a subjective experience involving body, soul, and spirit.

2. Worship involves more than just the human element. It is a mutual encounter of humanity and deity.

3. Worship is more than just a monologue with God.

It is a dialogue of the highest form of communion.

4. We enter worship after we have passed the gate of thanksgiving and gone through the courts of praise. Worship is entering the throne room of the Almighty (Psalm 100:4).

5. Worship is not merely light-hearted, ebullient jubilation. It is an experience of reverent adoration, humble obeisance, and holy veneration.

6. Worship is coming to an understanding of God's holiness, within our finite limitations. The holiness of God demands that "no flesh should glory in his presence" (I Corinthians 1:29).

In conclusion, let us bring what we have discussed in abstract terms down to common experience by using a hypothetical illustration. Suppose you walk into a church service one night, find a seat, and wait to be told what to do. The worship leader begins with the chorus "I Am Blessed." As you stand at his request and begin to force air through your vocal cords, you notice how tired you are. You begin looking forward to returning to a sitting position. The leader continues to sing with gusto and urges you to follow his example.

After singing the song three times you notice that the words say something about being blessed. That thought doesn't inspire you because you don't feel particularly blessed tonight. After all, the transmission went out in your car, your daughter is at home sick, and your son broke the neighbor's window today. Besides, you feel rather blasé. Yet you continue to sing by rote memory. Others around you are apparently enjoying themselves. Some are clapping and others have their hands lifted while singing with enthusiasm. In order not to look uncooperative, you join in.

THREE STAGES OF DIRECT MINISTRY

Psalm 100:4	Thanksgiving	Praise	Worship
Gate	Acknowledging what God has done	Confessing who God is	Entering God's presence
	God's goodness	God's greatness	God's holiness
	Attitude	Expression	Experience
	Human effort	Transitional	Human and divine
	Acknowledging God	Agreeing with God	Communion with God
	Acquaintance	Friendship	Fellowship

| | Court | Throne room |

Fig. 2

As the spirit of worship rises, you begin to feel convicted about your ungrateful attitude. You really do have a lot to be thankful for! Then, deliberately, you begin to sing the words, agreeing with the message of the song. Even though you are tired and frustrated, you force yourself to praise the Lord. Although, it is difficult at first, you genuinely begin to feel thankful. Your arms become lighter as they are lifted heavenward. Something inside of you begins to break up. You feel a release from that bound-up frustration. Suddenly, you are caught up in such praises that you feel you will burst with the joy of the Lord!

Those who can relate to this illustration are normal. We have two natures, the carnal and the spiritual. This dichotomy can cause a conflict when we begin to praise the Lord. The inward, or spiritual, man knows that he should praise and worship God, but sometimes the outward, or carnal, man does not want to do so. As a choice of our will, then, we must sometimes force the outward man to give thanks and praise.

If we continue to discipline our flesh and offer praises, we will eventually arouse our whole being. If we will lift our hands and sing praises, before long we will be praising God willingly with our whole being. Therefore, we should not wait until we feel like praising. We should make a decision to do so based upon what we know about our great God. The anointing and the emotion will come if we will offer the sacrifice of praise.

"Great and marvellous are thy works, Lord God Almighty; just and true are thy ways, thou King of saints. Who shall not fear thee, O Lord, and glorify thy name? for thou only art holy: for all nations shall come and worship before thee; for thy judgments are made manifest" (Revelation 15:3-4).

Notes

[1]Donald O. Bolander, *Instant Quotations* (Little Falls, NJ: Career Publishing, 1984), p. 30.

[2]John MacArthur, *Worshiping the Son of God* (Panorama City, CA: Word of Grace Communications, 1985), p. 101.

[3]Jack R. Taylor, *The Hallelujah Factor* (Nashville: Broadman Press, 1983), pp. 82-101.

[4]Robert Young, "Index-Lexicon to the Old Testament," *Young's Analytical Concordance to the Bible* (Grand Rapids: William B. Eerdmans Publishing Company, 1974), p. 1.

[5]Ibid., "Index-Lexicon to the New Testament," p. 57.

[6]Ronald Allen and Gordon Borror, *Worship: Rediscovering the Missing Jewel* (Portland: Multnomah Press, 1982), p. 16.

[7]*The Zondervan Parallel New Testament in Greek and English* (Grand Rapids: Zondervan Publishers, 1975).

[8]W. E. Vine, *Vine's Expository Dictionary of New Testament Words* (McLean, VA: MacDonald Publishing Company), p. 1259.

[9]William Wilson, *Wilson's Old Testament Word Studies* (McLean, VA: MacDonald Publishing Company), p. 414.

[10]Ibid., p. 294.

[11]Samuel Macauley Jackson, *The New Schaff-Herzoq Encyclopedia of Religious Knowledge* (Grand Rapids: Baker Book House, 1950), vol. V, p. 469.

[12]Taylor, pp. 82-102.

C H A P T E R 3

Causes For Worship

*T*he principle of cause and effect is observable in every area of life. For every happening, there is a cause, and for every action there is a resulting effect. This chain of events leaves a trail of evidence that can be easily followed. Detectives use this principle when solving a crime. Astronomers use it to project theories concerning the origin of the universe. Parents may even use the principle to determine who has been in the cookie jar.

There are many obvious causes to worship the Lord and innumerable good effects as a result. Worship has a reciprocating nature that perpetuates a healthy relationship with God. A life of worship is progressive and enriching. The more we worship the more reason we have to worship. The more we magnify the Lord the greater our perception and awareness of Him will become. As a result, the easier and more natural worship will be.

Let us first discuss the causes for worship. They are many. In this chapter let us consider some of the more obvious causes for worship.

Humans Are Worshipers

We are faced with so much mystery in our world. So many things cannot be explained, even in our modern age of discovery. The spark of life, the vastness of the universe, the instincts of the animal kingdom, and the complexity of the human brain all defy human pretentions as people reach for control of the world. The more we learn, the broader the base for learning becomes. The unknown is always just out of reach. Once one question is answered two more surface.

Sir Issac Newton, an English physicist and mathematician, discovered the laws of gravitation and went on to formulate the laws of motion and to discover calculus. He was a very intelligent man and contributed greatly to the science world. But at the end of his life his last words were, "I do not know what I may appear to the world. But to myself, I seem to have been only like a boy playing on the seashore, diverting myself in now and then finding a smoother pebble or a prettier shell than ordinary, whilst the great ocean of truth lay undiscovered before me."[1]

We must also accept our lack of perfection. Mistakes are human. The perfectionist is rarely relieved of his frustration as he blunders and fumbles his way through life. Humans hope and reach for the perfect government, the perfect monetary system, the perfect philosophy, the perfect machine, and the perfect educational system but never find them. When a person can admit his own imperfections, he has achieved a great virtue. Augustine said, "This is the very perfection of a man, to find out his own imperfections."[2]

We are also faced with our own mortality. The inevitability of death constantly stalks us as we struggle to survive. Our lives are delicately balanced on the wall of eternity. The slightest wind can upset the stability, plunging us into the dark unknown. George Sweeting once said, "The wood of man's cradle rubs against the granite of his tomb." Life is so uncertain, but death is so very certain! Even those who achieve wealth and fame and accumulate great knowledge must ultimately face their mortality. They must pass through the curtain of mystery called death.

When people realistically face their deficiencies, they reach out for an omniscient Being. They look for a God who possesses perfection. When they consider the vast unknown they reach for the One who is all knowing. They search for something, or someone, eternal.

This innate nature makes us worshipers. People of every era and culture have worshiped. Many people have not worshiped the true God, the God of the Bible, but in some form they have worshiped. Archaeologists have uncovered many ancient cities in which the temple was the largest building. Its location was in the center of the city, and it appeared that the inhabitants' whole lifestyle was centered around their religion. Throughout history humans have danced, offered sacrifices, conducted parades, built idols, given gifts, fasted, flagellated themselves, and even practiced human sacrifice in order to obtain favor with God.

This craving for God is not a learned desire; it is inherent. Isolated tribes of people who have had no contact with other communities of people have some form of worship. People worship because an inner drive compels them. Judson Cornwall observed, "In some way, not now fully explained, there exists a common denominator among all people of all times, and that generic force is worship. Worship is as universal to mankind as marriage."[3] The psalmist said, "Let every thing that hath breath praise the LORD. Praise ye the LORD" (Psalm 150:6). We human beings will worship something. God has created humanity with this inherent nature.

This intrinsic need to worship something is similar to the other basic human drives. Psychologists have identified several inherent drives in mankind such as the desires for food, sex, rest, and recognition. These drives are amoral in their God-given state, but in their attempts to satisfy these needs humans often use immoral methods. For example, nothing is wrong with the appetite for food unless we become gluttonous or eat things detrimental to our health. The desire to worship can also be polluted when people seek false gods and practice ungodly methods.

One of man's immoral practices over the years has been idol worship. In Bible times the Hebrews constantly dealt with idol-worshiping people. The Egyptians were idol worshipers. The Canaanite tribes worshiped idols. Even in the New Testament, the Greeks were idol worshipers. Idolatry is also practiced today in a more subtle form, in which people do not worship images of false deities but objects and concepts of modern ingenuity. The worship of materialism, ideology, sensuality, technology, or education has replaced primitive idol worship in many cases.

Another modern form of false worship is self-worship, currently known as secular humanism. At the heart of this false religion is the belief that mankind's natural ability will ultimately cure all the ills of the world. Humanists look to the unexplored reserves in the human brain as a source of unusual power, and they accept the theory of evolution as fact. Many humanists expect humans to take a quantum leap in the evolutionary process, becoming superpersons and perhaps even developing a sixth sense. In the final analysis, the secular humanist worships the human body and mind.

Even those who are detached from all religious activity, then, do not escape from the inherent human characteristic of worship. When they establish their priorities, something in their lives takes first place. Every person worships something. They might do so unconsciously, but nevertheless, they are loyal and committed to something, and that something is the master that rules every area of their lives.

It has often been said that there is a God-shaped void in every person's heart and only God can fill it. People search for God because they are incomplete without Him. They suffer from the Fall. Something is missing. They reach for something perfect, and only God is perfect. They long for something eternal, and God is the Eternal One. They long for omniscience and only God has perfect and complete wisdom. "Deep calleth unto deep" as a person reaches for something beyond himself (Psalm 42:7). Job said, "Oh that I knew where I might find him!" (Job 23:3).

We have a wonderful promise that if we will seek after the Lord we will find Him. "That they should seek the Lord, if haply they might feel after him, and find him, though he be not far from every one of us" (Acts 17:27). "He is a rewarder of them that diligently seek him" (Hebrews 11:6).

So much sin and false religion is a result of human efforts to satisfy this innate desire to worship. It is sad that so many people are looking in the wrong places for the wrong things.

Worship Harmonizes with God's Cosmic Scheme

The kingdom of God and the kingdom of Satan are diametrically opposed to each other. Every person alive is on one side or the other. We choose to align with the forces of God or the forces of Satan. Worship correctly positions God at the center of this universe. It acknowledges and proclaims Him as the Creator and Sustainer of all things. Worship brings the creation into harmony with the Creator. Worship acknowledges God to be exactly what He is, therefore harmonizing the worshiper with God's divine nature.

Worship helps to bring about the fulfillment of God's divine plan. It is a creative force energized by the Holy Spirit. Worship is a part of the spiritual growth process. As II Corinthians 3:18 states, "But we all, with open face beholding as in a glass the glory of the Lord, are changed into the same image from glory to glory, even as by the Spirit of the Lord." God is in the process of changing us to be like Him, and worship is a vital part of this transformation. Ern Baxter explained, "All worship has a creative aim, for it is a movement of the creature in the direction of ultimate reality. The creative aim of worship is the total transfiguration of the created order."[4]

God's prevailing order in this universe will ultimately subdue all opposing forces. His divine plan will be fulfilled. Worship positions us in a place of harmony with God's predominant authority. Worship puts us in a submissive role of self-denial before God (Mark 8:34).

Homogenization is a common process in our modern world that makes every particle of a substance the same size so that it blends smoothly. Not only is our milk homogenized, but many products are prepared with the same method. Peanut butter, cosmetics, and baby food are other good examples of homogenization. When we worship we are homogenized with God's purpose and essence. We become uniform with God's creation. Through worship, we blend heavenly things with earthly things in a harmonious way.

We must realize that sinful humanity and God are incompatible, and God does not change! If we are going to harmonize with God, then, we must do the changing. We must submit and bend in worship in order to unite with the divine character of God.

Worship Is Universal

Worship has been a prevailing practice throughout all time. It was habitual in heaven before the creation of humanity. Among God's probing questions to Job was, "Where wast thou when I laid the foundations of the earth? . . . when the morning stars sang together, and all the sons of God shouted for joy?" (Job 38:4-7). Why did angels sing and shout? They were worshiping God and expressing joy at God's marvelous creation. Worship has been the practice of every age. Although God's plan has progressed through many stages of development, worship has always been a vital part of God's program. Worship will always be a part of God's program, for worship is eternal.

Every glimpse of heaven in the Bible reveals worship.

Isaiah saw the Lord sitting upon His throne with seraphim crying, "Holy, holy, holy, is the LORD of hosts" (Isaiah 6:1-3). The twenty-four elders and the four living beings in John's vision were worshiping around God's throne (Revelation 4-5). In that scene, it appears that millions of angels joined in a song of praise, saying, "Worthy is the Lamb," and all creation joined the celebration of worship. "And every creature which is in heaven, and on the earth, and under the earth, and such as are in the sea, and all that are in them, heard I saying, Blessing, and honour, and glory, and power, be unto him that sitteth upon the throne, and unto the Lamb for ever and ever" (Revelation 5:13).

Humans are not the only created things that worship. Inanimate objects also offer a form of worship. The heavens are glad, the earth rejoices, the sea roars, the fields rejoice, and the trees sing as they offer praise unto the Lord (I Chronicles 16:31-33). The pastures and valleys shout for joy and sing (Psalm 65:13). "Let the floods clap their hands: let the hills be joyful together" (Psalm 98:8). "Let the heaven and earth praise him, the seas, and every thing that moveth therein" (Psalm 69:34).

Of course, nature does not worship God as people do. Nevertheless, all creation, in a natural and wonderful way, glorifies the Creator. We worship by choice; it is a decision of our will. Yet, in nature there is a universal compulsion to applaud the Creator. All of creation complies with the Creator in perfect accord, but humans are free agents. God's diversity, creativity, and grandeur are displayed through His creation as it conforms to God's divine order.

This function of nature is vividly illustrated by the

words of Jesus. As He rode into the city of Jerusalem, His disciples rejoiced and praised Him, but the Pharisees were unhappy with their response and asked the Lord to stop their praise. "And he answered and said unto them, I tell you that, if these should hold their peace, the stones would immediately cry out" (Luke 19:40). God is so great that if we do not praise Him nature will be compelled to take our place.

The Greatness of God

The more we learn about God the more overwhelmed we will become. Isaiah said his name shall be called "Wonderful," meaning full of wonder, or causing wonder (Isaiah 9:6). To wonder means to be stricken with awe and amazement, to be taken aback with surprise. The awesomeness of God compels us to worship Him. When we consider God, we are overwhelmed by His mystery, magnitude, and magnificence. God is the source and sustainer of all things. He is the epitome of all good virtues. He is perfect in every way. His phenomenal power is measureless.

Since God is the paragon of excellence and wonder, His greatness is a major cause for worship. Thomas Carlyle noted, "Wonder is the basis of worship."[5] God never ceases to be wonderful.

God is unique and separate from all others. No creature can compare with Him. His virtues, attributes, abilities, and accomplishments are universally unequaled. The psalmist said, "For the LORD is a great God, and a great King above all gods" (Psalm 95:3). Let us consider some natural and moral attributes of God that uniquely belong to Him.

Natural attributes of God. Certain eternal character-istics of God define Him as God in a natural way. For ex-ample, the raw power and ultimate control of God is seen in His omnipotence, omnipresence, and omniscience.

• *Omnipotence.* Perhaps the greatest demonstration of God's infinite power is creation. He made everything from nothing, just by His spoken word. Throughout the Word of God He is proclaimed as the Almighty. God is the primary source of all powers that exist in our world. He has no limitations except those He has imposed upon Himself. "For with God nothing shall be impossible" (Luke 1:37).

• *Omnipresence.* In Spirit form, God is everywhere. He dwells in every cubic inch of this vast universe, mak-ing it impossible to escape from His presence. "The eyes of the LORD are in every place, beholding the evil and the good" (Proverbs 15:3). His presence is like a pierc-ing light that nothing can stop, penetrating through everything, casting no shadows.

• *Omniscience.* God is the epitome of wisdom and knowledge. "Neither is there any creature that is not manifest in his sight: but all things are naked and opened unto the eyes of him with whom we have to do" (Hebrews 4:13). God knows the end from the beginning. Not only does He see what we do, but He sees the very thoughts and intent of our hearts.

Moral attributes of God. The moral attributes of God direct His natural powers, forming a perfect balance of the divine essence. Even though God can do anything He wishes, at any time He wishes, by definition He cannot act contrary to His own moral nature.

• *Love.* This inexplicable force is very elusive when

we try to define it with words. It is an emotion and it is
also a decision of the will. It is a fondness, an affinity,
an affectionate attraction, or a benevolent yearning
toward someone. God's love is the greatest love. His love
exceeds the love between husband and wife, friends, and
family members. God's love exceeds all human abilities
to love, for human love has limitations while God's love
is unlimited.

• *Truth.* Humans by nature search for reality. They
strive to differentiate between mind and matter, between
spirit and substance, between eternal laws and whims.
Pilate expressed this ancient quest at the trial of Jesus
when he asked, "What is truth?" (John 18:38). Pilate
never came closer to truth again, for Jesus, the epitome
of truth, stood before him (John 14:6). Knowing Jesus sets
people free from confusion in their perplexing search for
reality. "And ye shall know the truth, and the truth shall
make you free" (John 8:32). The life of Jesus Christ is
the perfect pattern to live by, and God's Word establishes
the eternal laws and ethics by which we should live.

• *Holiness.* The word *holy* in the Bible is translated
from the Hebrew word *qadesh* and the Greek word *hagios,*
which both mean "set apart" or "separated."[6] It also
means "pure, clean, sacred, separate from sin."[7] God is
unique and set apart in His holy state. He forms the
backdrop of perfection by which everything is measured.
Mankind is cumbered with faults and errors, but God has
none. God's holiness is a great focal point of worship.
Humans fall at His feet in utter helplessness when they
stand in the presence of the holy God. We must join the
angelic host and declare, "Holy, holy, holy, is the LORD
of hosts" (Isaiah 6:3).

71

The greatness of God is covered only in a brief way when we discuss these natural and moral attributes of His. Volumes can be written about the great virtues and characteristics of God. He is also revealed through compound names in the Old Testament such as Jehovah-jireh, "The LORD will provide"; Jehovah-rapha, "the LORD that heals"; Jehovah-shalom, "the LORD our peace"; and others.[8] Further study of these names of God's self-revelation give great cause to worship the Lord.

Many other titles in the Word of God metaphorically reveal glorious qualities in His character. Examples are Lion of the tribe of Judah, Lamb, bright and morning star, lily of the valley, captain of our salvation, dayspring, rock, vine, light of the world, door, and Alpha and Omega. Devotional books can be very helpful in expanding our understanding of God's greatness and our ability to worship.[9] Jack Taylor's book, *The Hallelujah Factor,* gives 230 biblical reasons to worship the Lord.[10]

God Seeks Worshipers

It is difficult for us to view things from God's perspective, due to our strongly humanistic society. We look at everything with humanity at the center—what we do, how we respond, and how we are affected. But in worship God is at the center. Worship begins with God and ends with God.

The woman at the well asked Jesus the debated question of the day. Samaria or Jerusalem—which was the correct place to worship? (See John 4:19-24.) Jesus explained that the important thing was not the place but that people worship in spirit and in truth, "for the Father seeketh such to worship him."

God seeks a love relationship with humanity. It may be difficult for us to imagine that God actually derives pleasure from our worship, but He does. Jesus said the first and greatest commandment was, "Thou shalt love the Lord thy God with all thy heart, and with all thy soul, and with all thy mind" (Matthew 22:37). If we love the Lord, worship will be a natural response.

There are compelling reasons to worship God. If we blind our eyes to His greatness and refuse to worship Him, someone else will. His excellent greatness prevails upon the world in such a forceful fashion that if people refuse to praise him the stones will cry out to laud the King of kings. (See Luke 19:40.)

Notes

[1]Clifton Fadiman, *The Little Brown Book of Anecdotes* (Boston: Little Brown and Company, 1985), p. 427.

[2]Donald O. Bolander, *Instant Quotations* (Little Falls, NJ: Career Publishing, 1984). p. 199.

[3]Judson Cornwall, *Elements of Worship* (Bridge Publishing: South Plainfield, NJ, 1985), p. 13.

[4]Ern Baxter, "Before the Throne," *New Wine*, October 1982, p. 21.

[5]Bolander, p. 278.

[6]Robert Young, *Young's Analytical Concordance to the Bible* (Eerdmans Publishing Company: Grand Rapids, MI, 1974), pp. 487, 488.

[7]William Wilson, *Wilson's Old Testament Word Studies,* (MacDonald Publishing Company: McLean, VA), p. 220; W. E. Vine *Vine's Expository Dictionary of New Testament Words* (MacDonald Publishing Company: McLean, VA).

[8]David K. Bernard, *The Oneness of God* (Word Aflame

Press: Hazelwood, MO, 1983), pp. 48-49.

[9]See, for example, Dick Eastman, *A Celebration of Praise* (Baker Book House: Grand Rapids, MI, 1984).

[10]Jack R. Taylor, *The Hallelujah Factor,* (Broadman Press: Nashville, TN, 1983), pp. 130-41.

Effects of Worship

*N*ow that we have identified major causes for worship, let us consider some major effects of worship.

God Is Gratified

We can become so preoccupied with receiving personal blessing that we rarely consider that we can actually give God pleasure. But according to God's Word, all things were created for his pleasure (Revelation 4:11). Although God is self-sufficient and has need of nothing, He still finds pleasure in our worship. He aggressively pursues our fellowship. He initiates fellowship by knocking at our heart's door (Revelation 3:20). Our worship is a response to His initial wooing.

Hebrews 13:15-16 exhorts us, "Let us offer the sacrifice of praise to God continually, that is, the fruit of our lips giving thanks to his name. But to do good and to communicate forget not: for with such sacrifices God is well pleased." Clearly, God finds great pleasure in our offering of sacrificial praises. He has said, "This people have I formed for myself; they shall shew forth my praise" (Isaiah 43:21).

Pleasing God should be our supreme desire. Worship will achieve that desire, for God is very gratified by our worship. That is why we have referred to worship as a direct ministry unto the Lord.

The Worshiper Is Edified

As chapter 2 has stated, worship is a mutual exchange between God and the worshiper. We begin by offering thanksgiving and praise unto the Lord, which lifts us into another dimension spiritually. In worship God lifts us out of our carnal world of problems and limitations into the spiritual realm, where the Spirit enables us to transcend what normally would bind our spirit and depress our emotions.

Several times in the Old Testament, when sacrifices were offered to God, fire fell from heaven to consume them (I Kings 18:38; I Chronicles 21:26; II Chronicles 7:1). If we will offer a sacrifice of praise unto the Lord, He will answer by the fire of the Holy Ghost. This fire will burn out the impurities of a contaminated, carnal life. It will purge us of the evil desires that try to dominate us. Real worship is very therapeutic to the human spirit.

There is much attention given today to self-improvement, success, and motivation. Success gurus are disciplining their followers with such techniques as psychotherapy, meditation, hypnosis, biofeedback, and numerous other pop psychological methods. Even Christian teachers have developed some of their own methodologies of achieving success and mental prosperity. Some television ministers are preaching the power of positive thinking, positive confession, and holistic medicine to assist human deficiencies.

The problem with many of these methods is that they are self oriented. But as Hunt and McMahon note, "Selfism is also at the heart of the entire success/motivation world. The Bible never urges self-acceptance, self-love, self-assertion, self-confidence, self-esteem, self-forgiveness, or any of the other selfisms that are so popular today. The answer to depression is not to accept self, but to turn from self to Christ."[1]

Worship is God oriented, in contrast to the psycho-therapist's humanism! Yet it is the most powerful mental health treatment available to humanity. As a result of the Fall, people desperately seek help to overcome their deficiencies. Worship is God's method of lifting them out of their quagmire of psychological kinks. In worship we think positively about God. We are brought into harmony with His divine scheme, which enables God to impart some of Himself to us. Through worship we become more Christ-like as we have fellowship with Him. Worship is the ultimate therapy in positive thinking and positive living.

Countless Christians have entered the church bowed down with the cares of life. Physically tired and mentally drained, they were edified through praise and worship. When they left the service they were strengthened and at peace about their problems.

Judson Cornwall, in his book *Let Us Praise,* told how breaking through to praise and worship for the first time affected his formal congregation. "It was lifting us out of a self- and need-centeredness, to a Christ-centeredness. There were other unexpected benefits of praise. It brought a new honesty into our midst. It helped us enlarge our concepts of God. In teaching us how to release our emotions of love and joy, it began to have a noticeable effect in our church's marriages and inter-personal relationships. It moved us from negative to positive attitudes. It changed our services from identification to participation. It began to mold our congregation into a family unit, for once we learned to flow love to God, we began to learn how to love one another."[2]

Praise unto the Lord is described in wonderful terms throughout the Bible. Terms such as "making melody," "laughter," "singing," "joyful noise," and "shout for joy" are used to describe the expressions of praise and worship. Lifting hands, clapping hands, dancing, leaping, playing music, and shouting are definitely not signs of a burdened down, confused, distraught worshiper. The Christian can find joy and strength in praise.

The power of praise was revealed in my own life in a very vivid way once. I was with my family in a motel room in Dallas, Texas, when I had a severe kidney-stone attack. The pain was almost unbearable. I paced the floor, took a hot shower, and writhed on the bed, but nothing helped. My wife called the paramedics, and they were available if we needed them. After over an hour of intense pain my endurance began to wear thin. I rolled on the bed in agony, begging God for relief. I was about to give up and go to the hospital when the thought came to me to praise the Lord.

This thought was very difficult for me. I debated it in my mind for some time. How could I thank God when I was in such pain? I almost resented God for allowing me to hurt so badly. After all, I was a minister of the gospel. I was his humble servant (at least when things were going well). Then I Thessalonians 5:18 suddenly came to my mind: "In every thing give thanks: for this is the will of God in Christ Jesus concerning you." Also I remembered that Paul said, "Giving thanks always for all things unto God" (Ephesians 5:20).

I began to thank the Lord in spite of the pain. In fact, I began to thank the Lord for the pain. I felt a tremendous rush of emotion when I forced my lips to praise. "Lord, I don't understand why I am having to hurt so badly. But I know that all things work together for ultimate good (Romans 8:28), and I thank you for it."

One moment I was in excruciating pain; the next moment I felt no pain whatsoever. God instantly stopped the pain! God allowed me to have that experience to teach me about the power of praise.

Obviously it does not always work that way in every case. If it did my new-found formula would drastically bite into the profits of every pharmaceutical company in America. God has a way of designing all His principles so that we must trust Him and not a formula. Nevertheless, this experience was a great blessing and has inspired me to praise Him always in all things.

Many times I have been in similar situations and God did not instantly cure the pain or remove the problem. Nevertheless, great strength can be gained in such circumstances through praise. We can take that "lemon" circumstance and "make lemonade" through praise. In the darkest night, praise will illuminate the stars in our world. When thorns prick us, praise will help us find the rose. The Lord wants to bless us if we will get on His wavelength. Praise will lift us up into the heavenly dimension where divine encounters are certain. David gave us a promise from the Lord: "Delight thyself also in the LORD; and he shall give thee the desires of thine heart" (Psalm 37:4). First we must praise Him!

Worship Aids in Evangelism

When I was a teenager, my friends and I used to play a trick to entertain ourselves. In a busy shopping mall we would begin to look up as if we saw something. As we pointed toward the ceiling and acted excited about something above, we would look askance at the crowd to see their reaction. Inevitably, others would also look up to see what we were looking at. Seeing nothing, most people would move on and ignore us, but others would continue to search as they walked along, hoping not to miss the excitement.

Our excitement was contagious. Even though we were only faking, still people fell for it. Likewise, praise and worship will have a strong effect on others. As we look upward, lift our hands upward, and speak praises upward we will cause others to get involved in the "upward." Making much ado over Jesus will cause others to consider Him. The intensity of our worship will work to convince the sinner of our sincerity.

A life of consecration and discipleship will influence the world in a powerful way. Living a godly life will influence our nation and community much more than just adhering to a philosophy. Through our Christian character we fulfill our role as the salt of the earth (Matthew 5:13). We exert a preserving influence for morality in our world. The role of discipleship should not be made second place to any form of Christian service. At the same time, seeking to have discipleship without worship is dead legalism. Worship adds life to our commitment.

When the sinner sees us enter into real worship, he is convinced that we do not live as Christians just to avoid the lake of fire or to receive some reward. He begins to understand that we are not adhering to a creed out of sheer habit or will power. Instead, the worshiper is in love with Jesus Christ! He is not just following a staid tradition or using the church as a social outlet. The true worshiper loves the Lord with all his soul, mind, and strength. He enjoys God. Worship confirms to the world that being a Christian is a pleasurable experience.

The world is filled with religion. Cults abound that teach false doctrines to satisfy the spiritual needs of people. But no religious group enjoys their god like true Christians enjoy the true God. We do not base our faith on a God-appeasing premise, but the basis of our faith is a God-loving relationship.

Our worship also generates a powerful spiritual atmosphere. The Lord inhabits our praises (Psalm 22:3), and as a result, sinners are drawn by His love. Jesus said of Himself, "And I, if I be lifted up from the earth, will draw all men unto me" (John 12:32). He was plainly speaking of the death He would die at Calvary, yet there is great significance in the lifting up and the drawing. The simple splendor of the Cross compels people to consider Him; thus when we draw attention to Jesus Christ and the Cross by our worship, people will be drawn to Him.

Worship generates a spiritual energy that grips the hearts of men and women. Our worship is a magnetic force that attracts people to Jesus. A friend of mine was drawn by this worship-created conviction. His truck route brought him past a worshiping church every day. When he would pass he would look at the building and sign and something within him would be drawn to the church. As the days passed the feeling to attend the church became stronger. He had never been witnessed to by any of the members, yet he felt a longing to attend a service. He finally checked the schedule of services and made plans to visit. The end result was that he was saved and became a minister of the gospel.

A sinner who visits a worshiping church will feel the convicting power of God. Sometimes, in our zealous efforts to convert sinners, we can make them feel like a helpless worm exposed to a hungry bird. There is definitely a time to exhort people to make a decision for the Lord. There is also a time for travail and intercession. Certainly, they will appreciate our concern for them if they understand our motive. But sometimes we only need to worship! Worship creates the climate for the moving of the Spirit. It will move people who would be untouchable through human effort. Jesus said, "No man can come to me, except the Father which hath sent me draw him" (John 6:44). Human efforts have their limitations but God has none. "Not by might, nor by power, but by my spirit, saith the LORD of hosts" (Zechariah 4:6).

Spiritual Battles Are Won

God's people have always had battles to fight. David, Israel's great king, laid down his sword long enough to pick up his harp and lead his people in a psalm of praise: "Let the high praises of God be in their mouth, and a two-edged sword in their hand" (Psalm 149:6). Israel's victories were characterized by "praise in the mouth" as well as the "sword in the hand." It is important to realize that praise is still an effective weapon against the enemy. A praising church will be a victorious church!

One of the most vivid examples of the effective weapon of praise is found in II Chronicles 20. King Jehoshaphat received the disheartening news that Judah was about to be invaded by an army of Ammonites and Moabites. The king called a fast and prayed desperately for God's intervention. After the people fasted and prayed, the Lord spoke through the prophet Jahaziel comforting words of certain victory. They praised and rejoiced because of their faith in the words of the prophet.

Jehoshaphat organized the strangest military formation imaginable. Instead of placing the mightiest warriors at the front of the troops, he put the singers there. They were instructed to praise the Lord with these words: "Praise the LORD; for his mercy endureth for ever" (II Chronicles 20:21).

As they began to sing and praise the Lord, the armies of Moab, Ammon, and Mt. Seir began fighting among themselves. Their fighting became so intense that every soldier was killed. When the Israelites surveyed the valley from the watchtower, they saw a multitude of corpses. Not a single enemy escaped! The Israelites rushed to the battlefield to collect the loot. It took them three days to gather all the spoils of war.

What a weapon our praises can be! If we will follow Jehoshaphat's example, our enemy can be destroyed by the power of praise. Satan likes to tempt us when we are down. Self-pity is the natural response when things are not going our way. But praise will drive away depression and we will become glad, even when our circumstances

83

are not good.

God and Satan both desire our worship. God wants our worship because He is worthy and He desires our loving fellowship. Satan wants our worship because he hates us and wants us to destroy us. Pride was the cause of Satan's expulsion from heaven, for Satan wanted the worship that only God deserved (Isaiah 14). Therefore, through praise and worship we join the conflict of the ages and become warriors in God's army. Nothing makes it more clear whose side we are on than does worship, for whom we worship we serve.

When Jesus was tempted in the wilderness, Satan came three times to tempt the weaknesses of the flesh. Jesus responded, "Thou shalt worship the Lord thy God, and him only shalt thou serve" (Matthew 4:10). When Jesus let Satan know in no uncertain terms that as a man He was determined to worship God only, Satan left Him alone. Praise will make the devil more uncomfortable than anything we can do.

When we put on the whole armor of God, let us not forget to put on the "garment of praise" (Isaiah 61:3). In our Lord's first mention of the church he made it clear that we will be in a battle but also that victory would be ours: "Upon this rock I will build my church; and the gates of hell shall not prevail against it" (Matthew 16:18). What an assurance that the battle will be won! But we will only participate in that victory when we lay down the playthings of the flesh and take up the weapon of praise.

Our churches must be vibrant with praise. We must take up our swords and march forward like an army determined to crash through the gates of hell. Praise and worship will rally the troops and frighten the enemy. And no weapon that is formed against us shall prosper (Isaiah 54:17).

Worship Opens the Door
to the Supernatural

Lift up your heads, O ye gates; and be lift up, ye everlasting doors: and the King of glory shall come in. Who is this King of glory? The LORD strong and mighty, the LORD mighty in battle. Lift up your heads O ye gates; even lift them up, ye everlasting doors; and the King of glory shall come in. Who is this King of glory? The LORD of hosts, he is the King of glory (Psalm 24:7-10).

This psalm was probably written soon after King David had begun his eventful reign. The nation had regained its national pride, and the ark of God was returned to its rightful place. The priests were once again conducting the sacred rituals. It was a time of celebration for the nation of Israel. It could be that this psalm was used when the ark was returned to the city of Jerusalem.

Some theologians believe that this song was sung in two choruses. In other words, as the entourage of worshipers reached the gates of the city of Jerusalem one group would sing, "Who is this King of glory?" Then the second group of singers would cry out, "The LORD strong and mighty, the LORD mighty in battle." Alternating as they sang, they worshiped as a joyous marching choir.[3] The huge gates of the city were lifted and the ark was brought through the opening, amid shouts of praise and singing.

This beautiful psalm is somewhat mysterious due to its adaptability to various great events in God's glorious agenda. It appears that this prophetic song can apply in several different ways.

First, of course, is the historical purpose just described. Second, it can apply to the resurrection of Jesus and His deliverance of the redeemed saints of the ages. After Jesus defeated Satan and took the keys of death and hell, He led captivity captive (Ephesians 4:8-10). The psalm can be seen as representing His triumphant resurrection, ascension, and entrance into heaven. Third, the psalm could apply to the entrance into the New Jerusalem by the Lord and His saints after the Great Tribulation and Battle of Armageddon.

The fourth application of this psalm is a spiritual one. In order for the church today to enter into the blessings of God we must enter His courts with praise and thanksgiving (Psalm 100:4). Our praise will open the door to the presence of the Lord. As we stand at the door of spiritual opportunity and demand that the door be opened, we will be challenged. If we will proclaim the Lord to be the King of glory, the Lord strong and mighty, we will see the doors open. Our praise will become a powerful spiritual force to open new doors in the Holy Spirit. We can receive healing, deliverance, protection, and guidance through the power of praise.

Notes

[1]Dave Hunt and T. A. McMahon, *The Seduction of Christianity* (Harvest House Publishers: Eugene, OR, 1985), pp. 193, 195.

[2]Judson Cornwall, *Let Us Praise* (Logos International: Plainfield, NJ, 1973), p. 27.

[3]C. H. Spurgeon, *The Treasury of David* (MacDonald Publishing Company: McLean, VA), vol. I, p. 378-79.

CHAPTER 5

Pseudo Worship

*I*n 1887, a grocery clerk waited on a man buying produce at her store. She noticed that the twenty-dollar bill he used to make the purchase was unusual. The ink came off in her hand! She tried to suppress her concern since she knew the customer was Emmanuel Linger. He was a respectable elderly gentlemen who had patronized the store for years.

Later she called the police to examine the bill, and they determined it indeed was a counterfeit. After searching Mr. Linger's apartment, the police found in his attic tools for making the bills: an easel, paint, and brushes. A very skillful artist, he was counterfeiting the twenty-dollar bills by painting them by hand.

Also in the attic of his apartment they found three portraits. Later, at a public auction, these three paintings sold for over sixteen thousand dollars, an average of over five thousand dollars each. The ironic thing is that Emmanuel Linger was spending about the same amount of time on the counterfeit twenty-dollar bill as on the five-thousand-dollar portrait. He stole from the public in small amounts and from himself in large amounts.

In a similar way, Satan tries to misdirect the children of God into pseudo worship. He understands the potential within believers when they enter into true worship. Since worship is so valuable, Satan wants to trick the worshiper into producing a counterfeit. He tries to delude the worshiper with a substitute that has very close resemblance to the real.

The intensity and fervor of religious activity does not confirm its validity. Misdirected efforts can be very costly. When we offer up counterfeit worship we not only shortchange God but we also miss many blessings that could be ours.

Due to carnal human nature, it is a constant battle for us to keep Jesus at the center of our worship. We can become preoccupied with music, methods, programs, personalities, trends, and movements to the point of moving Jesus from the center of our activity. We can even worship these diversions. Ironically, we can even worship the way we worship!

There is nothing inherently wrong with the potential diversions mentioned. They can be tools and accessories to worship. As long as they are just accompaniments to worship they can contribute to the worship experience. But noise and activity that does not put Jesus at the center is not worship.

To define worship better and to disclose some pitfalls, let us look at what worship is *not*.

Response to Music
Worship is not physical and emotional response to

music. Music has always played a prominent role in the worship of God. The Old Testament method of worship included choirs and orchestras extolling psalms of praise. Music is also a vital ingredient in Christian worship. Many churches have full-time ministers of music who arrange a variety of orchestrated numbers to inspire worship. One church spent $350,000 on a P.A. system to insure the highest quality of musical sound.

Bob Larson made this observation about music and Christianity: "I have had the privilege of traveling to more than seventy countries around the world. As a student of religions, I have been able to make many valuable observations regarding the impact that belief systems can have on a culture. One of the more obvious conclusions I have drawn is that no religion outside of Christianity has so generously incorporated music as a means of expression. Even the heathen and agnostic must admit that the greatest music of human history owes a debt of inspiration to the Christian faith."[1]

Music's ascendancy in our churches demands that we understand more thoroughly this melodious force. We recognize that music has psychological and emotional effects and is used quite extensively by the secular world. Let us use the following analysis to separate the fleshly from the spiritual.

My family and I were returning from vacation and making the long drive home. We were tired and the two children were restless in the back seat. The agitation was mounting between them as we drove along, and it looked as if I would have to follow through on some of my threats to get them to settle down. I turned on the radio and tuned in some classical music. About fifteen minutes later I noticed a tranquility had settled upon the back seat. I said to my wife, "Help me remember this trick."

We have all experienced the mesmerizing effect of soft, symphonic music. At the other extreme, we all at times have unconsciously allowed our foot to become too heavy as we joyously drove down the highway listening to a lively gospel tape. Music is a mood setter. It has an inexplicable effect on human emotions.

This principle is illustrated in the Bible. David, a great musician, was called to Saul's palace to provide music for the raging king. David's music was an antidote to Saul's fits of rage (I Samuel 16:14-23).

It is important not to confuse the feelings that music can produce with the move of the Holy Ghost. We must not confuse our response to music with worship. H. H. Farmer, an English theologian, said he was a little afraid of great organ music because he thought some people mistook the trembling of an organ pipe for a visitation of the Holy Spirit.[2]

A lady explained to me that her home church had a very gifted organist and many talented musicians and singers. She visited a small church that was limited in the music department, and it was halfway through the service before she realized she was not worshiping. In her frustration she became cognizant of her problem: there was no organ. After returning home she began to observe her worship responses more closely. She discovered that the organist was actually controlling her worship with the swells of sound.

There is certainly nothing wrong with organs and other instruments of music. They contribute immensely to a worship service. Our expression to God must be motivated by a deep love and appreciation for Him, however. If we had no music could we still worship demonstratively and readily with the same intensity of expression? We should not wait for certain sounds to raise us to a familiar emotional high before we begin to praise God. If we have great music, let us praise Him! If we have no music or poor music, let us praise Him still!

It is also important to understand that worship and praise involve action. Just sitting and listening to beautiful music is not worship. Far too frequently, artistic performances draw more attention to the performers than to Jesus Christ. Enjoying a performance objectively is fine, but it should not be substituted for worship.

No musical instrument should be viewed as an "instrument of worship" per se. Musical instruments assist in worship, but worship is not mechanical or inanimate. The first mention of musical instruments in the Bible is Genesis 4:21, which states that Jubal was the father of all who play the organ and harp. But Adam and Eve and their family worshiped God before this time, before the invention of musical instruments.

Music is intrinsic within the believer. Those who are in love with Jesus have a song in their hearts. External musical stimulus is not necessary when the song is within. Instrumental music is secondary to the inherent melody of heart. "Be filled with the Spirit; speaking to yourselves in psalms and hymns and spiritual songs, singing and making melody in your heart to the Lord" (Ephesians 5:18-19).

Crowd Response

Worship is not the excitement of a crowd. I learned while a student in a large high school the power and contagious atmosphere of a crowd. The school was very active in football, and pep rallies were conducted before every game to build school spirit. The pep squad would do their routine as the band played their loud numbers. Cheerleaders chanted slogans, students waved large signs, and other students performed skits representing the destruction of our opponents. Ultimately the climax came. The gymnasium swelled with clapping, stomping, music, and shouting. The adrenaline began to flow in the veins of hundreds of excited students who were convinced of victory.

During the height of one of these high school pep rallies, I heard timbers cracking behind me. Due to the intense stomping, the top bleacher had broken. A large, splintered board fell to the floor with a crash as the students struggled to maintain their balance. The rally was so noisy that only those in the immediate area even noticed the destruction.

In such gatherings every person is brought to a uniformity of mood. Excitement permeates the atmosphere. It is almost as if an invisible current electrifies every molecule in the building. The individual is engulfed and almost coerced into conformity with the crowd.

Sociologists explain this mysterious power in the following way: "Crowd behavior takes many forms: a screaming audience of teenagers gathered to watch their current idol; a lynch mob; a rioting crowd burning and looting stores; a panic-stricken crowd fleeing from a disaster; a cluster of spectators watching the aftermath of a street accident. It originates in milling, restless, random movements that stimulate others to behave similarly, release energy, and communicate various possible meanings in an undefined situation."[3]

It is easier to worship in a crowd of worshipers than by ourselves, and to facilitate worship is one of the purposes for Christians coming together. For most of us, it is in large gatherings of worshiping Christians that we experience some of the greatest joys of communion with God. Our gathering together for church services, camp meetings, conferences, crusades, and rallies is ordained of God (Hebrews 10:25). In the midst of this activity, however, there is an element of the physical and psychological. Therefore, it is imperative that the worshiper be sincere and allow the crowd to intensify his personal focus on Jesus Christ.

During a large worship service it might be good to ask ourselves, "Is Jesus at the center of this meeting? Are my own expressions pure worship to God?" Our demonstration should be God motivated and not crowd motivated.

The benchmark for true worship is the centrality of Jesus Christ. We worship the King and not the kingdom. Just being swept along with the crowd to sing, clap, or demonstrate in some particular fashion—just to parrot those around us without keeping Jesus in focus—is not true worship.

We need enthusiasm in our worship! The Greek roots of the English word *enthusiasm* are *en* and *theos,* meaning "in God."[4] What an accurate term to describe God-centered worship by hundreds of singing, rejoicing worshipers!

Some gatherings are charged with excitement and anticipation from the beginning of the service. The praises of hundreds of voices lifted in unison are inspiring and exhilarating. The unity is potent as the praises rise like a mighty force. When such meetings are God centered, the gathering becomes the seeding ground for the miraculous. Healings, deliverance, salvation, and other miracles will result when we allow our unity and mass praise to lift us into God's presence.

Heaven would not be complete without the host of worshiping redeemed ones. "After this I beheld, and lo, a great multitude, which no man could number, of all nations, and kindreds, and people, and tongues, stood before the throne, and before the Lamb, clothed with white robes, and palms in their hands; and cried with a loud voice, saying, Salvation to our God which sitteth upon the throne, and unto the Lamb" (Revelation 7:9-10). Nevertheless, it is not crowd excitement, but the united focus on God, that produces true worship.

Response to Personality

Worship is not attraction to a charismatic personality. During the height of the "Beatle mania" that swept the United States during the 1960s, Rosemary, a student in my high school class, was a devoted fan. She had a wealthy aunt in Arizona who had the honor of entertaining the Beatles at her ranch during an American tour. Rosemary's aunt sent her a cigarette butt that was supposedly dropped by Ringo Star, the drummer for the Beatles. She carried it in a small glass case, neatly resting on a bed of cotton. Rosemary was the most popular girl in school for several weeks. Just to get a glimpse of this treasure was a delight to every student in the school. I even took a peek myself.

It is a characteristic of the adolescent to become infatuated with personalities. Teens often have their idols plastered on the walls of their room and dream for hours about the fantasy world of rock stars, sports heroes, and movie stars. The sad thing is, many adults never graduate from this stage of hero worship. This fixation with glamorous personality continues to affect their priorities into adulthood. Their idols may change, but they continue to have a hero-worship mentality.

At times it seems that the church world is also intrigued with sports heroes, music stars, and famous personalities. When such people are guests at a service, the attendance swells to record numbers. It seems that if someone famous supports a certain church or religious event, then it must be God ordained!

The church must take precautions against creating folk heroes among us. Obviously, there are people in the church who are gifted with magnetic personalities. There are ministers who are gifted with the silver tongue of an orator. The anointing of God is upon them, and they speak eloquently and persuasively. God has blessed the church with gifted musicians who are highly skilled. Their music blesses and edifies. These special people are gifts to the church. They should be respected and given opportunities to minister to the body of Christ. But we must not allow infatuation with personalities to rise among us and overshadow the supremacy of the Lord Jesus Christ. We do not gather to be entertained by the talents of gifted people. The aura of charismatic personality should not be mistaken as the moving of the Spirit.

Worship is a celebration! We are the celebrants, and the Lord Jesus is the celebrity. The celebrity is not to be upstaged by other personalities. Whether we are in the pulpit or in the pew, we are all celebrants. Nothing should draw attention away from Him. No participator in worship should steal the spotlight that belongs to God.

My brother was a guest speaker at a rally in which a lady was baptized in the Holy Spirit. Several months later he saw her at another meeting and thought she would be glad to see him. He made his way over to speak to her, but to his amazement, she did not remember him. Later, as he pondered over what he had done wrong, the Lord spoke to him and said, "You did well! You led her to Me and not to you!"

If we are not careful, our meetings will feature so many important people that we can become disoriented. We should give honor to whom honor is due. Nevertheless, too much "stroking" can be harmful. Those who deserve recognition will appreciate brief, concise compliments that are offered sincerely. Our premium effort of extolling and praising should be for the God of this universe. Our praise to God can never be overdone as long as it is offered sincerely.

If we are only motivated in a service when a favorite speaker or singer is ministering, we have a problem. There is only one personality who deserves our worship—Jesus Christ! If He is not central, our excitement will be pseudo worship.

Church Attendance

Worship is not just attending church. Across America every Sunday morning, sleepy-eyed audiences sit in front of lighted boxes called televisions. With slippers on their feet and coffee in their hand, they sip relaxingly, wrapped in their robes. They snuggle up to their favorite televangelist to get a little conscience soothing. They are the "electronic church."

As isolated observers they are plugged in to a little religion. Their contact with Christianity is electronic and artificial. They have become part of a smug, contented Christendom that is satisfied just to look through the window and not become involved. Being only observers, it is impossible for them to get involved in a worshipful experience. They watch others sing, pray, preach, and worship.

One of the reasons for such great success among televangelists is that most denominational church services are just a performance by a few. The congregation assembles to sit in a detached and passive manner. They watch and listen to a handful of people do religious things. Therefore, staying at home and watching a televised church service instead of actually attending a service is not really very different. They would not have become involved at church anyway, since most churches do not permit the congregation to praise much. And plugging into the electronic church requires a lot less time and energy. In most cases the televised program is more professional and entertaining.

We are living in an entertainment-crazed society. North Americans in particular feel that entertainment is one of the great needs of life. There are a myriad of enticing thrills to excite the senses. Technology and the entertainment industry have produced a society of people who expect to be served with pleasurable delicacies by just the push of a button or turn of a knob.

The church is overwhelmed when it attempts to compete with the entertainment industry. People have come to expect the best in entertainment. The church cannot compete, nor does God expect it to do so. But it can provide a place for Christians to come together, interact with one another, and commune personally in worship. People are hungry for relationships, fellowship, and communion. The church service should be a place for people to find freedom of participation and active involvement. It should be a real world of humanity and deity coming together in concord.

Just attending a church meeting is not the worship that God expects. Thanksgiving, praise, and worship require action. Some people think that just showing up for the meetings is all they need to do. Just making it to the job each day requires effort and action, and an employer certainly desires for his employees to have good attendance. But after an employee makes it to work, he must do something! So should we do something at church.

Robert E. Webber wrote in his book, *Worship Is a Verb,* "We must let go of our entertainment expectations and remind ourselves that we are not in church to watch a Christian variety show. We have gathered together in worship to be met by God the Almighty. God, the Creator of the universe, the One who sustains our lives, our Redeemer and King, is present through proclamation and remembrance. He wants to communicate to us, to penetrate our inner self, to take up residence within us. And as we go through the experience of meeting with Him in this mystical moment of public worship, we are to respond."[5]

Worship is not a spectator sport, nor is it entertainment. We have not worshiped sufficiently just by attending a meeting; God desires and expects our active participation. "Thou shalt love the Lord thy God with all thy heart, and with all thy soul, and with all thy mind. This is the first and great commandment" (Matthew 22:37-38).

Aesthetics

Worship is not aesthetic appreciation. A young family took a vacation to the southwestern part of the United States, taking along grandparents who had just retired from farming. As they stood overlooking the Grand Canyon, everyone made delightful comments about its beauty. They were overwhelmed with the variety of colorful hues and the magnitude of this vast gorge. They noticed that Grandpa wasn't saying anything, however. They soon learned his silence was not a result of awe when he said, "You can't grow much corn here!"

He was blinded to the beauty by his utilitarian outlook. But some things in life are void of any practical usefulness. Their only contribution to life is their beauty.

It is a wholesome thing to recognize the extravagance of God's creation. God has been very lavish in His adornment of this world with beauty. Colorful flowers will blossom and yield their sweet fragrance in remote parts of our world and never be seen by the human eye. The sea has unusual creatures living in its depths that are not even identified yet. God has created stars and galaxies by the millions just to add glitter to our sky. We are enveloped in a world of diversity and beauty. There must be a God behind all this beauty, complexity, and order. "The heavens declare the glory of God; and the firmament sheweth his handywork" (Psalm 19:1). "The fool hath said in his heart, There is no God" (Psalm 14:1).

Yet we must not worship creation, but the Creator.

As we thrill at the beauties of nature, we must remember, "For thou has created all things, and for thy pleasure they are and were created" (Revelation 4:11). All our adoration must go to God, who is the source of all things. Worship is deeper than just enjoying God's marvelous creation. Worship is enjoying communion and fellowship with the Creator of all these wonderful things.

Paul pronounced judgment upon those who worship the creature more than the Creator (Romans 1:25). Creation worshipers change the truth into a lie, and as a result they are perverted in their thinking. A preoccupation with nature can lead to a belief called pantheism, which teaches that God is not a person but merely the laws, forces, and manifestations of nature. What a distortion of the truth!

God has gifted certain people with the ability to construct beautiful things of artistic value. Their contribution has resulted in some very beautifully designed sanctuaries. Vaulted ceilings, chandeliers, plush carpet, glass, stone, and special lighting have provided outstanding places of worship. Some churches are so beautiful that they have become architectural showpieces.

Our churches should be nice, and we should strive for excellence in our efforts for God. The beauty should remind us of His glory and majesty. Nevertheless, we must exercise caution along these lines, considering historical examples. Some of the most outstanding architectural wonders were constructed in times of great apostasy. "The lesson which seems to require constant rediscovery is the fact that worship is not primarily a state-of-the-art but rather a state-of-the-heart."[6] Beautiful aesthetic surroundings do not generate God-centered worship, although they can help to create the mood for worship.

Cheerleading

Worship is not response to a cheerleader. In most sporting events today there are two groups of people who assist the teams: the coach and his staff and the cheerleaders. From these two roles we can draw an interesting analogy to the worship leader and make several instructive applications.[7]

• *Coaches motivate a team; cheerleaders are a team of their own.* The sole responsibility of a cheerleader is to keep the audience making noise. They offer no contribution to the actual strategy of the game. The coach, on the other hand, is concerned with making things happen to win the game. He does not do much physically, but his influence is direct and effective regarding the game on the field. The cheerleaders put on a show themselves, independent of what is happening on the playing field. Essentially, the cheerleaders are a self-contained unit.

The apostle Paul was not interested in the rah-rah circuit. He declared that his footsteps were deliberate and purposeful: "I therefore so run, not as uncertainly; so fight I, not as one that beateth the air: but I keep under my body, and bring it into subjection: lest that by any means, when I have preached to others, I myself should be a castaway" (I Corinthians 9:26-27).

• *Coaches are flexible; cheerleaders are programmed.* A coach may have a game plan ahead of time, but he is open to change in his strategy as the game progresses. Cheerleading, on the other hand, is a memorized pattern. It consists of beautiful, precise, symmetrical, well-executed routines. It is very attractive and entertaining at the first of the season, but after several games the

101

cheers and routines become artificial and sometimes banal.

Worshipers of God know that methods are not sacred even though the gospel is. They are not attached to routines that have become archaic and ineffective. Scoring at the goal line is their chief objective. Quality worship should be our goal, by whatever means is most effective.

• *Coaches have a place for silence: cheerleaders panic over silence.* The coach must concentrate on the game, and he requires time for serious contemplation. At times a player will be discouraged, and the coach will put a hand on his shoulder or give him a pat on the back. He knows when words are unnecessary. Cheerleaders are only concerned with noise making. They feel that noise is proof of their success.

A worshiper knows that there are times of stillness and sensitivity. He knows that worship is not a monologue of noise. Worship is a dialogue of communion with God. "Be still, and know that I am God: I will be exalted among the heathen, I will be exalted in the earth" (Psalm 46:10).

The worship service can fall into the trap of the cheerleading game when making noise becomes the objective. A misdirected worship leader can prod an audience with challenges and actually build a crescendo of noise that is only an empty echo to his own words. Hand clapping and shouts can be just a response to cheerleading, and the people can amuse themselves with a game of group exercise.

True worshipers do not wait to be prodded or coerced into praise. They come to a service poised to praise and worship. "Enter into his gates with thanksgiving, and into his courts with praise: be thankful unto him, and bless his name" (Psalm 100:4).

Being the worship leader is a delicate responsibility. The best thing the leader can do to inspire worship is to worship himself. Worship is contagious. People come to church tired and frustrated by the cares of life and need a leader who can inspire them to praise God. It is not always an easy job. The leader must stimulate their thoughts toward God. If the worshipers can see Jesus, they will be inspired to praise Him. "Praise ye the LORD. Praise God in his sanctuary" (Psalm 150:1).

Religious Phrases

Worship is not repetition of religious phrases. In my private devotion, I asked the Lord to help me to become a better worshiper. The Lord told me I was restricted in my ability to praise. My vocabulary was too limited, and many expressions I was using were hackneyed. My repertoire of praise expressions was limited to about five: "Praise the Lord"; "Hallelujah"; "Glory"; "Thank God"; "Praise your name." These words of praise when offered sincerely are great tools of expression. But my continual use of them made them bland and lacking in freshness.

When I began to look for other words and expressions, I found the Bible to be full of praise vocabulary. It is shameful that we limit our expressions to a few old standbys, when God is so magnificently glorious. So many titles are available to describe His excellence. He deserves the best we can offer, not only in sincerity but also in effort and creativity.

There are heights of worship when words are not necessary. Yet as we make our approach into praise, having a well informed mind about God will contribute greatly to our worship experience. The more we know God, the greater worshipers we become.

The third commandment says, "Thou shalt not take the name of the LORD thy God in vain" (Exodus 20:7). The word *vain* means empty, meaningless, or even false. The name of God was regarded with great sanctity by the Hebrew scribes. In fact, they even refused to pronounce the sacred name. When they wrote it they used careful procedures in order not to desecrate the name of the Lord.

In the New Testament, God revealed Himself by the name of Jesus. His name, through faith, is a spiritual weapon to use against our enemy (Luke 10:17). In fact, everything we do in word or deed is to be done in the name of Jesus (Colossians 3:17).

Indiscriminate use of this sacred name could cause us to become careless. Perhaps we could even be guilty of using God's name in vain. In worship we should not use sacred words carelessly. Sometimes expressions pour forth absentmindedly from our lips and are nothing more than vain babbling. Jesus warned about such carelessness when He said, "But when ye pray, use not vain repetitions, as the heathen do: for they think that they shall be heard for their much speaking" (Matthew 6:7). Our words of praise must be deliberate. They must be intelligible to our spirit and mind and must come from a heart of earnest sincerity.

We need to expand our power of expression by studying God's Word. As we read the Bible we will learn fresh and exciting things about the Almighty. Many expressions of praise that are very powerful and laden with meaning can be taken out of God's Word. Adding new expressions to our worship vocabulary will add freshness to our worship. And we can pay careful attention so that the old, familiar words and phrases never lose their meaning.

We have discussed seven areas in which our religious activity can become pseudo worship. These are sensitive areas, and sometimes the real can be almost indistinguishable from the fake. But by putting forth conscious efforts to improve our worship, we can expand our potential for greater spiritual blessings.

Notes

[1]Bob Larson, *Rock* (Wheaton, IL: Tyndale House Publishers, 1980), p. 99.

[2]John Killinger, "Preaching and Worship, the Essential Link," *Leadership,* vol. 1, 1986, p. 125.

[3]John Biesanz and Mavis Biesanz, *Introduction to Sociology* (Englewood Cliff, NJ: Prentice-Hall, 1969), p. 447.

[4]*Webster's New World Dictionary of the American Language,* 2nd ed. s.v. "enthusiasm."

[5]Robert E. Webber, *Worship Is a Verb* (Waco, TX: Word Books, 1985), p. 114.

[6]Ronald Allen and Gordon Borror, *Worship: Rediscovering the Missing Jewel* (Portland: Multnomah Press, 1982), p. 23.

[7]Dean Merrill, "Beyond Cheerleading," *New Wine,* March 1985, pp. 12-13.

CHAPTER 6

Methods of Worship: Physical Expressions

worked in the drafting profession for a number of years and learned that methods of procedure can become a very opinionated subject. Once the supervisor was leading a new applicant around the drafting room to show him our operation. As they moved about the room, the eager young man stopped at a table where a draftsman was busy shading his drawing with a red pencil. The arrogant young man sneered and said, "Who ever heard of shading with a red pencil; everyone knows you shade with blue!" Perhaps he felt he would make points with the supervisor by pointing out this error. The amusing thing was, it did not matter what color was used. The reproduction of the drawing would not be in color, so it did not matter. Red was just as good as blue! Instead of making a good impression, the young man revealed a glaring flaw in his perception. He was lacking in the ability to keep the objective ahead of the method.

We can become so preoccupied with the *modus operandi* of worship that we forget the objective. The

Samaritan woman at the well was very concerned about where to worship, but she was not worshiping at all. It is easy to become preoccupied with methods, procedures, trends, and formalities to the point of losing track of the real purpose. Keeping the purpose ahead of the program is always a challenge.

In this chapter let us discuss methods of worship. Such a discussion must not be isolated from the rest of the book. If we just learned methods of worship and did not allow our love for the Lord to motivate us, our worship would be legalistic and mechanical. All methods of worship are good if they achieve the end result: exalting the Lord Jesus Christ! No method is of value if it does not minister to the Lord.

Methods of worship vary according to geographical location, customs in a particular group, and differences in individual personality. Some denominations practice communion every week but do very little singing. Others make music their major expression and neglect the Eucharist altogether. A survey of worship methods of modern Christianity reveals that almost every denomination has its own liturgical guidelines. Their methods often become sacred cows that they guard with great religious pride. They usually close the door to any fresh methods by saying, "We've always done it this way!"

What Is Our Standard?

Is there any standard for worship methods? Are we free to do just what we think is acceptable or what is traditional? As in all other areas of Christian doctrine and practice, the Bible is the source of guidance in this matter. The Bible is replete with worship methods. These methods are not peculiar to a certain generation or culture but are appropriate for every age. Styles and trends come and go, but human nature has been the same for ages. Biblical worship methods are based on human nature and the will of God. Therefore, they never cease from being effective.

The Old Testament and the New Testament are the source of worship methods. Some think the Old Testament is just extra baggage when it comes to instruction about worship. Of course, the ceremonial law of the Old Testament is no longer in force. But the principles still apply, and furthermore, worship is an eternal practice. There was worship in heaven before the world was formed (Job 38:4-7). In every preview we get of heaven in the future we find worship around the throne of God (Revelation 4; 5; 15; 19). Worship is not something we can relegate to a particular age. Neither can we restrain expression in worship by permitting only certain biblical methods and excluding others.

The New Testament does not describe worship methods as abundantly as the Old Testament. The reason is that now we enjoy a relationship with God not known under the law. Therefore, we do not need as much instruction in the mechanics of worship. The born-again believer naturally becomes a worshiper. His worship should be the spontaneous result of a love for God, without coaching. The young groom does not have to be sent to a seminar to be taught how to kiss his bride. Some things just come naturally.

In summary, worship methods should be sincere and should have biblical support. Moreover, all true worship requires surrender to the guiding presence of the Holy Spirit. Instead of focusing primarily on the outward expressions of worship, we must entertain the presence of the Holy Spirit. A failure to understand this truth causes much of the pseudo worship that is prevalent today.

Striving for Balance

The first lesson I learned when I began to drive was to stay between the ditches. On the road to worship, tradition is one ditch and excessive experimentation is the other.

Tradition has its place of benefit in worship, but it is not so sacred that we should become locked into a form. Becoming ritualistic with our worship will destroy the freshness. The word *new* is used in the Bible more times with *song* than with any other word. God does not necessarily want something new, but He wants something fresh. A new song will provoke a fresh look at old truth. As the old saying goes, "Variety is the spice of life."

On the other hand, constant variation in service schedules and worship methods can also become frustrating. There is no virtue in keeping a congregation on edge by the unpredictable. Constant change can become a distraction from the real purpose of praise and worship. People will become preoccupied with learning and adapting. Worshipers usually cannot worship with a new song until they have learned the words and melody fairly well. Therefore, constantly pushing people with new methods will only frustrate. The key is to have enough consistency so that new things will have a positive impact.

In discussing methods of worship, let us first consider physical expressions. Our bodies are our greatest offering of praise to the Lord. We have the ability to make noise and to demonstrate physically with our bodies. Our emotions are heightened when we express them in some physical fashion. When a child jumps up and down at the sight of his first bicycle, the joy he feels is intensified by the freedom of expression. If the child were forbidden to show any emotion, it would dull his sense of joy and excitement. Likewise, our love for the Lord and our joy in Him should be expressed. Physical expression is natural and necessary. Our bodies are the temple of God; therefore we are to "glorify God in your body, and in your spirit, which are God's" (I Corinthians 6:20).

Let us divide physical expression into four groups: the mouth, the hands, the feet, and the whole body.

The Mouth

The mouth is the greatest tool of praise and worship. Speaking is the most sophisticated and thorough way we have of revealing what is in our mind. Bodily movement can express some things, but with language the mouth can express the abstract and the complex. The mouth is the most frequently used physical method of praise.

Our mouth can praise and worship God in the following ways:

1. *Talking.* Saying things about God in a deliberate and purposeful fashion can be praise. Speaking intelligible statements about God's glory and confirming all the things the Lord has said about Himself plays a great role in praise and worship. We can tell others or tell the Lord directly of His greatness. Talking implies a controlled, low-keyed, intellectual verbalizing of God's greatness.

• *My tongue also shall talk of thy righteousness all the day long* (Psalm 71:24).

111

• *I will meditate also of all thy work, and talk of thy doings* (Psalm 77:12).

• *Make me to understand the way of thy precepts: so shall I talk of thy wondrous works* (Psalm 119:27).

2. *Shouting.* Sometimes we are so excited about the Lord that we shout His praises with a loud voice. Shouting is an expression of extreme joy and excitement. Most people raise their voice from time to time in response to situations in life, either in a negative or positive way. We see in the Scriptures that it is an appropriate method of expressing praise also.

• *Shout unto God with the voice of triumph* (Psalm 47:1).

• *And the Levites . . . stood up to praise the LORD God of Israel with a loud voice on high* (II Chronicles 20:19).

• *And when he was come nigh, even now at the descent of the mount of Olives, the whole multitude of the disciples began to rejoice and praise God with a loud voice for all the mighty works that they had seen* (Luke 19:37).

• *And I beheld, and I heard the voice of many angels round about the throne and the beasts and the elders: and the number of them was ten thousand times ten thousand, and thousands of thousands; saying with a loud voice, Worthy is the Lamb that was slain to receive power, and riches, and wisdom, and strength, and honour, and glory, and blessing* (Revelation 5:11-12).

3. *Singing.* We can chant or sing words of praise to music or a rhythm. The words and music can be written

or extemporaneous. More will be said about this method in chapter 9.

• *Sing praises to God, sing praises: sing praises unto our King, sing praises* (Psalm 47:6).

• *All the earth shall worship thee, and shall sing unto thee; they shall sing to thy name. Selah* (Psalm 66:4).

• *And when they had sung an hymn, they went out into the mount of Olives* (Matthew 26:30).

• *And at midnight Paul and Silas prayed, and sang praises unto God: and the prisoners heard them* (Acts 16:25).

• *I will declare thy name unto my brethren, in the midst of the church will I sing praise unto thee* (Hebrews 2:12).

4. *Laughing.* This universal human expression is a sign of joy and delight. Some think that all activities in the church should be solemn and void of any humor. But laughter can be very expressive and therapeutic. In fact, Martin Luther said, "If you're not allowed to laugh in heaven, I don't want to go there."[1]

• *When the LORD turned again the captivity of Zion, we were like them that dream. Then was our mouth filled with laughter, and our tongue with singing* (Psalm 126:1-2).

• Seven times the psalmist says, *"Make a joyful noise unto the LORD,"* or the equivalent. (Psalm 66:1; 81:1; 95:1-2; 98:4, 6; 100:1. Laughing is a joyful noise!

5. *Speaking in tongues.* Some churches today forbid

their people to speak in tongues, but Paul very plainly said, "Forbid not to speak with tongues" (I Corinthians 14:39). Forbidding tongues is a plain and obvious violation of Scripture. Praise and worship in tongues is an experience available to everyone. (See Acts 2:4, 38-39.) A person who is baptized with the Holy Ghost will enter into worship and ascend to a level of interaction with God that goes beyond human language. Speaking in tongues is a supernatural, God-given utterance by a person caught up in praise and worship. (For further discussion, see chapter 7.)

• *For he that speaketh in an unknown tongue speaketh not unto men, but unto God* (I Corinthians 14:2).

• *For if I pray in an unknown tongue, my spirit prayeth, but my understanding is unfruitful. What is it then? I will pray with the spirit, and I will pray with the understanding also: I will sing with the spirit, and I will sing with the understanding also* (I Corinthians 14:14-15).

• *But ye, beloved, building up yourselves on your most holy faith, praying in the Holy Ghost* (Jude 20).

The Hands

The hand is a very important part of the human body. It is our tool of giving and receiving. Lifted hands are a sign of surrender, while the clenched fist is a sign of rebellion or violence. The handshake is a gesture of goodwill the world over. Waving the hand is a sign of greeting. The deaf use a language that is almost totally the work of the hands. This versatile part of our anatomy has a unique shape, with every individual having an identifying fingerprint. Artists find the hand difficult to draw due to its delicate design.

The hands are mentioned in the Bible more than any other part of the body (including the heart). The laying on of hands symbolized the transfer of blessing from one generation to another in the Old Testament (Genesis 48:13-20). Similarly, in the New Testament the laying on of hands symbolizes the transfer of spiritual blessing or authority (Acts 6:6; II Timothy 1:6). The "hand of the LORD" is a frequently used phrase in the Bible that refers to His presence and His influence.

Our language uses the word *hand* when referring to the work force. We all understand the expressions "Give me a hand," and "We are shorthanded." The hand represents the active part of our bodies that does the work.

Since the hands are such an important part of life they should also be used for praise and worship.

1. *Lifting of hands.* Lifting hands is a sign of surrender. It reveals empty and unthreatening hands as they are held high over the head. It is also a sign of reaching, not reaching outward but upward to the Lord. Lifted hands also form a symbolic funnel for receiving a blessing from heaven.

• *I lift up my hands toward thy holy oracle* (Psalm 28:2).

• *Thus will I bless thee while I live: I will lift up my hands in thy name* (Psalm 63:4).

• *Lift up your hands in the sanctuary, and bless the LORD* (Psalm 134:2).

• *And Solomon stood before the altar of the LORD* . . .

115

and spread forth his hands toward heaven (I Kings 8:22).

• *I will therefore that men pray every where, lifting up holy hands, without wrath and doubting* (I Timothy 2:8).

2. *Clapping of hands.* Clapping the hands together is a universal symbol of approval. Applause is offered to those who please us. Unfortunately, the heroes of the world get more applause from humanity than our Lord does. Our ovation for the Lord should not be superseded.

• *O clap your hands, all ye people* (Psalm 47:1).

• *Let the floods clap their hands: let the hills be joyful together* (Psalm 98:8).

• *For ye shall go out with joy, and be led forth with peace: the mountains and the hills shall break forth before you into singing, and all the trees of the field shall clap their hands* (Isaiah 55:12).

The Feet

It might seem humorous to some that feet could be used in worship. Yet it is scriptural to stand, leap, run, and dance as expressions of praise. Let us examine the following verses of Scripture as they relate to praise.

1. *Standing.* We stand to show honor. Standing indicates alertness and full consideration. It also indicates availability and willingness to serve.

• *My foot standeth in an even place: in the congregations will I bless the LORD* (Psalm 26:12).

• *Behold, bless ye the LORD, all ye servants of the LORD, which by night stand in the house of the LORD* (Psalm 134:1).

• *Praise ye the LORD. Praise ye the name of the LORD; praise him, O ye servants of the LORD. Ye that stand in the house of the LORD, in the courts of the house of our God, praise the LORD* (Psalm 135:1-3).

2. *Running and leaping.* These actions are extreme expressions of joy and excitement. They are mentioned a few times in Scripture in connection with exceptional blessings or miracles. I once saw in the newspaper a picture of a man caught in midair by the photographer as he was leaping from the front porch of an old dilapidated house. His mouth was wide open in a wild whoop, and his legs were stretched out in an uncoordinated fashion. The caption told of his recent winning of over a million dollars. No doubt the readers smiled with understanding at such behavior.

• *And he leaping up stood, and walked, and entered with them into the temple, walking, and leaping, and praising God. And all the people saw him walking and praising God* (Acts 3:8-9).

• *Rejoice ye in that day, and leap for joy: for, behold, your reward is great in heaven* (Luke 6:23).

• *For thou art my lamp, O LORD: and the LORD will lighten my darkness. For by thee I have run through a troop: by my God have I leaped over a wall* (II Samuel 22:29-30). (See also Psalm 18:29.)

3. *Dancing.* People have expressed their feelings in all times and in all countries by rhythm and body movement. Dancing, as with other human expression, has been used for good and for bad. There is a worldly dance that

117

flirts with sexual infidelity and entertains sensual passions. Some religious cults think that their ceremonial dancing will bring magic powers. Dancing is one of the oldest arts and continues to be popular today.

Along with this diverse use of dancing in human culture, the Bible speaks about dancing in worship. Let us consider the following scriptural examples of dance as a worship method. (More will be said about worship dancing at the end of this section.)

• *Let them praise his name in the dance* (Psalm 149:3).

• *Praise him with the timbrel and dance* (Psalm 150:4).

• *And David danced before the LORD with all his might* (II Samuel 6:14). (See also I Chronicles 15:29.)

• *And Miriam the prophetess, the sister of Aaron, took a timbrel in her hand; and all the women went out after her with timbrels and with dances* (Exodus 15:20).

The Body
Expressions that involve the use and positioning of the whole body, namely bowing, kneeling, and prostration, seem to communicate less celebration and more adoration and humility before the Lord in worship. They transcend praise and climax in deep worship.

1. *Bowing and kneeling.* In North America people do very little bowing or kneeling. The Orientals are well-known for bowing in gracious greeting. The bow is a gesture of honor, submission, or appreciation. Kneeling is a more extreme expression of similar sentiments. Kneeling before another person symbolizes total submission,

even a pleading for acceptance in humble subjection. Thus, bowing and kneeling are particularly appropriate in times of intense worship.

• *For this cause I bow my knees unto the Father of our Lord Jesus Christ* (Ephesians 3:14).

• *O come, let us worship and bow down: let us kneel before the LORD our maker* (Psalm 95:6).

• *And I bowed down my head, and worshipped the LORD, and blessed the LORD God of my master Abraham* (Genesis 24:48).

• *And David said to all the congregation, Now bless the LORD your God. And all the congregation blessed the LORD God of their fathers, and bowed down their heads, and worshipped the LORD* (I Chronicles 29:20).

• *Now when Daniel knew that the writing was signed, he went into his house; and his windows being open in his chamber toward Jerusalem, he kneeled upon his knees three times a day, and prayed, and gave thanks before his God, as he did aforetime* (Daniel 6:10).

• *And when they were come to the multitude, there came to him a certain man, kneeling down to him, and saying, Lord, have mercy on my son* (Matthew 17:14-15).

2. *Prostration.* On a number of occasions in Scripture people fell down to worship God. These verses may not always mean that the people lay flat on their faces in a prostrate position; some could mean that they fell on their knees with their faces to the ground. In any case this position expresses similar feelings as bowing and kneeling, but with even greater intensity. It symbolizes

119

the epitome of humility, submission, vulnerability, and self-sacrifice. Prostration puts us as low and as close to the earth as physically possible.

• *And when they were come into the house, they saw the young child with Mary his mother, and fell down, and worshipped him* (Matthew 2:11).

• *And, behold, there cometh one of the rulers of the synagogue, Jairus by name; and when he saw him, he fell at his feet* (Mark 5:22).

• *And it came to pass, when he was in a certain city, behold a man full of leprosy: who seeing Jesus fell on his face, and besought him, saying, Lord, if thou wilt, thou canst make me clean* (Luke 5:12).

• *And suddenly there shined round about him a light from heaven: and he fell to the earth, and heard a voice saying unto him, Saul, Saul, why persecutest thou me?* (Acts 9:3-4).

• *And when I saw him, I fell at his feet as dead. And he laid his right hand upon me* (Revelation 1:17).

Worship Dancing

Pentecostal churches have practiced worship dancing for many years. Due to the growth of the Pentecostal movement, more attention has been given to the practice of dancing in worship. Many denominations feel it is extreme and out of place in a church service. Even some Pentecostal churches have questioned its biblical basis. Let us take a more detailed look at this controversial method. Is it a legitimate method of praise and worship? Should it only be an extemporaneous expression or does choreography have a place in worship?

Is dancing a biblical method of praise and worship?
It is obvious that dancing is a biblical method of praise
and worship. Seven places in the *King James Version* the
word *dance* is used in direct reference to worshiping the
Lord (Psalm 30:11; 149:3; 150:4; II Samuel 6:14; 16;
I Chronicles 15:29; Exodus 15:20). The Hebrew words
used here are *machol* (dance, dancing, chorus), *karar* (to
dance, move around), *raqad* (to dance, skip), and *mecholah*
(dance, dancing, chorus). Studies in the original languages
make it even clearer that dancing is an appropriate expression. Some Hebrew and Greek words connote or im-
ply a form of dance but are not translated as "dance" in
the *KJV*.

Hebrew

English Transliteration	Meaning	Times Used
gil	circle in joy, dance	29
pazaz	leap	1
sagaz	play, dance	4
alatz	leap	5
samach	spontaneous emotion of extreme happiness expressed in some visible, external manner	150

Greek

English Transliteration	Meaning	Times Used
chairo	relates to the Hebrew words *samach, gil,* and *alatz*	28

skirtao	leap with joy	3
allomai	leap	1
choros	circle dancing	1
agalliao	leap	10

Should worship dancing be involuntary or voluntary?
"Dancing in the Spirit" is an old-time Pentecostal phrase used to describe a physical movement brought about when the Spirit comes upon a person. The phrase is never used in the Bible, although it can be understood as scriptural when one accepts the reality of God's supernatural power moving upon someone who is engaged in worship. The worshiper dances involuntarily or without consciously directing himself, according to the orchestration of the Spirit.[2] We could also call it "anointed dancing." A person who dances in the Spirit is yielded to the Holy Spirit's control and will react in a variety of ways. They, perhaps, will shake, tremble, or even appear drunken. (See Psalm 2:11; Acts 2:13, 15.) The anointing in worship lifts the worshiper into an experience of ecstasy in which he is carried beyond just willful acts of demonstration, but his expression is assisted by the Holy Spirit.

Some have described their experience as a sudden surge of power going through their body like electricity, or as a warm sensation starting in the extremities and encompassing the entire body. Others have felt their skin tighten, forming goose bumps and causing their hair to stand on end. Sometimes the anointing simply brings an overwhelming feeling of intense joy, causing the whole body to feel light and buoyant. When a person has such an experience, his response will vary according to his personality.

"Dancing before the Lord" is a phrase sometimes used to describe a voluntary dance unto the Lord as an act of spontaneous, joyful praise in accordance with the Word of God. As such it is similar to hand clapping, although it signifies a greater level of intensity and should be used accordingly. As a comparison, singing and shouting with a loud voice are both scriptural, but the latter is a more intense expression and is used with that in mind.

"Dancing before the Lord" is less intense than "dancing in the Spirit." To use our technical definitions, it is more a praise expression than worship. A worshiper might begin to dance as a sacrifice of praise and an expression of joy and then find that the anointing of the Spirit leads him into "dancing in the Spirit."

It is scriptural both to "dance in the Spirit" and to "dance before the Lord." This lively expression will not be comfortable for everyone. In a service where dancing occurs, those who do not choose to dance should not be made to feel less spiritual. There are other methods of praise that are just as effective. And, regardless of how we label or define it, all worship dancing should be a sincere spiritual expression and should be led by the Holy Spirit.

Should worship dancing be extemporaneous or structured? In recent times structured dancing has become a practice with some groups, originating primarily among independent charismatic churches.[3] Structured dancing can be a rehearsed presentation by an individual or group of individuals. Sometimes it is a corporate performance by the congregation. In either case it is planned and organized. The question is, Is this true worship?

Those who are actually involved in the presentation can possibly be worshiping, but those who watch are more in a position to be entertained than to worship. Although structured dancing may seem similar to a musical performance that glorifies the Lord, it involves certain drawbacks or negative aspects that music alone does not have.

First of all, dancing is used by the world extensively for sensual purposes. Choreographed dancing aligns itself closely to the worldly use of dancing. Thus, this method could deteriorate very quickly into a sensual parade of the flesh. With the problems of immorality that have already confronted many churches, from the pulpit to the pew, this type of activity would not help efforts to appear above reproach. The clothing worn and the movements of the dance would require constant caution. In short, structured dance originated in a preoccupation with entertainment in American society. The church should never try to compete with the world as an entertainment center with theatrical pageantry.

Second, structured dancing would undermine our stand against worldly dancing. The church has taken a stand against worldly dancing (even though some types of folk dancing are not very harmful). The stand we have taken has been a preventive effort. The old saying is true: "Give the devil an inch, and he will take a mile." Even though in some circles it is in vogue to flirt with worldliness under the guise of a freedom from legalism, some liberties are not worth taking when we consider the gamble. Some things may not be inherently wrong but the disadvantages outweigh the benefits. Abstaining from structured dancing in worship is a wise exercise of Christian choice.

Third, body movement is a very limited method of communication. The purpose of structured dancing is to convey, in a dramatic way, worshipful truth. Choirs and other vocal music can communicate a clear and comprehensible message with words, but dancing cannot. Adding words to choreography would perhaps heighten the impact, but is it worth opening a Pandora's box of complications (i.e., maintaining proper dress, restricting certain movements and positions, upsetting traditional worship methods, bringing more entertainment into the church, finding people who have skills fitting for such activity, etc.)?

Finally, a study of the biblical examples of worship dancing and their historical and cultural setting indicates that worship dancing in the Bible was a spontaneous dance of joy or, at most, the use of traditional folk forms in an unrehearsed, freely expressive way. There is no scriptural precedent for choreographed or performance dancing as worship.

Another dance practice sometimes used today is "partner dancing," in which two or more people are in physical contact with one another. As they hold hands or express unity by some other means they dance together. Although this dance does not have a scriptural basis explicitly, the Jews have used such a dance at least since medieval times. They are known for the *hora*, a group dance that apparently originated in Eastern Europe. In this dance, several people form a circle with their hands on one another's shoulders, shuffle their feet, and kick in unison as they move in a circular motion.

Clearly, partner dancing would not be acceptable between men and women, for then it would focus more on interaction between the sexes rather than praise to the Lord. It would violate scriptural bounds of propriety, create a wrong impression for onlookers, and open the door to temptation. (See I Corinthians 7:1-2.)

The following story is a sad illustration of the destructive effects of dancing with partners of the opposite sex. A church in suburban Seattle began to practice intimate dancing. While at an elder's retreat, the pastor of this church had an experience while dancing with some of the ladies of the congregation. He claimed an overpowering experience of spiritual love as well as a mystical encounter with a dancing angel. He began dancing lessons at the church to teach others how to have this new experience, which he called a "connection." More and more couples began to experience "connections" as they danced with someone else's mate.

Christianity Today described how these sessions were conducted in 1987: "More than 1500 flock to the modern sanctuary several times a week for meetings lasting hours. Women bring dance slippers for sessions extending late into the night. Special rooms are set aside for intimate dancing. During worship services, unmarried couples commonly hold hands, rub shoulders, stroke hair, and kiss (not on the lips)."[4]

Predictably, married parties began to fall in love with partners with whom they had so-called "connections." One former member said that two dozen couples had begun divorce proceedings as a result of this new teaching. Eventually much immorality resulted, even among the leadership, and the church split.

It is the pastor's responsibility to see that things are done decently and in order. (See I Corinthians 14:49.) He should not allow dancing or any other physical expression to become excessive, unbalanced, or a display of carnality. Care should be taken not to allow the flesh to poison a true move of God.

Notes

[1]Laurence J. Peters, *Peter's Quotations,* (New York: Bantam Books, 1977), p. 285.

[2]See David Baird, "The Dance and Corporate Worship: The Positive View," *Ministries Today,* Jan./ Feb. 1988, p. 59.

[3]T. Burton Pierce, "The Dance and Corporate Worship: The Negative View," *Ministries Today,* Jan./Feb. 1988., p. 61.

[4]Ronald Enroth, "A Pastor Claims Dancing, Hand-holding in the Church Are Part of a 'Move of God,'" *Christianity Today,* 8 Aug. 1987, p. 32.

C H A P T E R   7

Methods of Worship: Enactments

*L*et us now discuss enactments as methods of worship. By enactments of worship we mean the practice of acting out certain landmarks of the Christian faith. In this type of worship we retell the gospel story by collective demonstration in language and drama.

We perform enactments in our everyday lives by celebrating birthdays, weddings, national holidays, ribbon cuttings, normal greetings, and anniversaries. Shooting fireworks on the Fourth of July and eating Thanksgiving turkey with all the trimmings are examples of enactments of celebration in everyday life. In the Christian faith we have dramatic enactments that help us express our relationship with God.

The Hebrews in the Old Testament practiced enactments such as the seven feasts (the greatest of them being the Passover), the Sabbath, worship in the Tabernacle, and the year of jubilee. These special days and rituals acted out their faith, giving it meaning and attaching it to historical events. The New Testament worshiper will find such enactments as communion, footwashing, baptism, hymns, special days, and preaching to be a source of rich meaning in worship.

Let us divide enactments into two areas, language and drama. We have already discussed some of these subjects relative to physical expression, but we will mention them again in connection with reenacting the gospel message.

Enactments through Language

1. *Scripture.* Reading, studying, meditating on, memorizing, and quoting Scripture is an integral part of private devotion. Reading or quoting Scripture can also be very beneficial in corporate worship. Some churches use Scripture readings to open a service or responsive readings during the service.

In addition to Scripture itself, most denominations use creeds, or summary statements of doctrine. Unfortunately, creeds tend to enshrine and perpetuate doctrines and traditions that are unbiblical. Since the Bible is our sole authority for doctrine, we should use it rather than creeds in our devotion and worship.

The Bible itself contains summary statements of doctrinal truth. For example:

> *Christ died for our sins*
> *according to the scriptures;*
> *and that he was buried,*
> *and that he rose again the third day*
> *according to the scriptures*
> (I Corinthians 15:3-4).

God was manifest in the flesh,
justified in the Spirit,
seen of angels,
preached unto the Gentiles,
believed on in the world,
received up into glory
(I Timothy 3:16).

Other passages that make condensed statements of faith or express fundamental truths can also be selected. When memorized, these passages of Scripture can be a great blessing in worship, recited by the congregation or by individuals.

Most Christian organizations have statements of faith or articles of faith. They express the basis upon which the members agree to have fellowship and work together, but rightly understood and used, they have no authority independent of the Bible itself. They express an understanding and agreement as to what the Bible teaches, but they are not tools for worship, objects of faith, or sources of doctrine. In this way they differ from creeds as traditionally used.

2. *Hymns.* Singing was definitely a part of New Testament worship. Beginning with Old Testament roots and continuing with the ministry of Jesus, psalms, hymns, and songs were a vital part of worship. Paul admonished the Ephesians, "Speaking to yourselves in psalms and hymns and spiritual songs, singing and making melody in your heart to the Lord" (Ephesians 5:19). (See also I Corinthians 14:15; Acts 16:25; Colossians 3:16; James 5:13.)

A song puts an amplitude to our words of praise.

131

Amiel said, "Music is harmony, harmony is perfection, perfection is our dream, and our dream is heaven."[1] When a worshiper is filled with the Holy Ghost, God puts a song in his heart (Ephesians 5:18-19). The songs we sing are just expressions of the song of the heart. A song attests to the transcendence of God in a way that nothing else will.

"In the New Testament the distinction between speaking and singing was far less pronounced than it is today. Neither Hebrew nor Greek had a separate word for singing in distinction from speaking."[2] But it is clear from the passages of Scripture previously cited that the apostolic church sang and composed songs. In Acts 4:24, "they lifted up their voice to God with one accord, and said . . ." Then follow several verses of beautiful praises. It appears that some of these words of praise were the words to a hymn. If so, this would explain how the group could lift their voices in one accord and pray these words together. In any case, great spiritual results followed this lifting of praise: "The place was shaken where they were assembled together; and they were all filled with the Holy Ghost" (Acts 4:31).

3. *Preaching and teaching.* Preaching and teaching are not exactly the same. (Preaching is reaffirming known information, proclaiming, and exhorting, whereas teaching is imparting new information and expounding. Preaching tends to appeal to the emotions more than teaching does.) Nevertheless, they both recreate the gospel story and provide the listeners with an opportunity to become involved. Preaching and teaching tell the story of God's dealings in the past and apply them to the present. Peter's message at Pentecost is a good example (Acts 2).

Here again the New Testament church is built upon the pattern of the Old Testament. The Book of Deuteronomy is a good example of preaching. The prophets also used this method to warn and to exhort. Jesus both taught and preached.

The pulpit ministry should inspire worship. Apostolic preaching was alive and powerful. It is shameful that some preaching is boring and does not inspire. Woodrow Wilson said, "One of the proofs of the divinity of our gospel is the preaching it has survived."[3] Unanointed preaching is an indictment against modern preachers. Peter's message at Pentecost resulted in three thousand converts being filled with the Spirit. His preaching in Acts 10 resulted in Cornelius's household receiving the Spirit. Peter and John "taught the people, and preached through Jesus the resurrection," and five thousand were converted (Acts 4:2, 4). Stephen's sermon to the Jewish council cut them to the heart and made them so angry they gnashed on him with their teeth (Acts 7). On and on the examples could go. The conclusion is that apostolic preaching moved people. When preaching or teaching exalts the Lord it can be defined as worship.

4. *Speaking in tongues.* Paul's teaching to the Corinthian church is rich with insights into the apostolic worship service. Speaking in tongues was definitely a part of worship in the early church. This supernatural utterance was used in basically three ways. First of all, speaking in tongues was the initial sign of the baptism of the Holy Ghost (Acts 2:4; 10:45-46; 19:6). Second, it was a method of private communication with God that edified the believer (I Corinthians 14:2-4, 14). Third, tongues was a gift of the Spirit used to edify the church when inter-

133

preted (I Corinthians 12:10; 14:5, 13, 27-28).

Paul certainly did not disparage or teach against speaking in tongues, but he taught the proper use of this supernatural expression. He was quite clear in his endorsement of tongues: "I would that ye all spake with tongues" (I Corinthians 14:5). "I thank my God, I speak with tongues more than ye all" (I Corinthians 14:18). "Forbid not to speak with tongues" (I Corinthians 14:39).

Tongues and worship go together. Those who spoke in tongues on the Day of Pentecost spoke "the wonderful works of God" in many languages (Acts 2:11). Cornelius and his household spoke in tongues and magnified God (Acts 10:46). Speaking in tongues is one of the highest experiences of communion with God that a person can have. In fact, worship is a key to receiving the Holy Ghost, which is evidenced by speaking in tongues. If a person has repented, worship will open the door and throw out the welcome mat for the Holy Spirit to enter.

Speaking in tongues is worship when it is an expression directly to God of praise and adoration. Messages of tongues with interpretation are a ministry of edification to the church and support the preaching and teaching of the gospel, whereas devotional tongues minister to God and to the individual believer (I Corinthians 14:2-5). When a believer prays and worships in tongues, he speaks directly to God. His spirit prays (I Corinthians 14:14). Paul concluded, "I will pray with the spirit . . . I will sing with the spirit" (I Corinthians 14:15). Private devotional tongues are important expressions of worship unto the Lord that reenact the initial experience of receiving the Holy Spirit, and tongues with interpretation reenact the gospel message.

Enactments through Drama

Drama reenacts historical events through the medium of visual, tangible, and concrete symbols. In one sense, all of the physical expressions of praise and worship that we have already discussed earlier could be considered drama. But by enactments through drama we specifically mean ceremonies or expressions that usually involve a group of people and portray a historical event.

1. *The Lord's Supper.* The Passover was the fulcrum of Old Testament rituals, and the Eucharist replaced it as a Christian enactment. "For even Christ our passover is sacrificed for us" (I Corinthians 5:7).

Jesus instituted this memorial at the Passover supper with His disciples (Matthew 26:26-29). The fruit of the vine is symbolic of His blood, and the bread is symbolic of His broken body. The apostolic church continued this memorial. It became a tradition among early believers and later was practiced by the Gentile church (I Corinthians 11:23-26).

The frequency of the Lord's Supper is not indicated in Scripture, although the Passover, from which it was derived, was celebrated once a year. The early Christians probably celebrated the Lord's Supper more frequently, in anticipation of the Lord's soon return. If practiced too often, it could lose its significance for people. Paul simply said, "For as often as ye eat this bread, and drink this cup, ye do shew the Lord's death till he come" (I Corinthians 11:26) Some groups practice communion more often than others. The important thing is that it be meaningful and contribute to worship.

Participating in the Lord's Supper has two primary purposes. First of all, it stimulates our memory to reflect upon the redemptive work of our Lord. Jesus said, "This do in remembrance of me" (Luke 22:19). When we reflect upon what Jesus Christ did at Calvary, we are motivated to faith and thanksgiving. The Greek word *eucharistia,* from which we get the English word *Eucharist,* means thankfulness or gratitude.[4]

Second, eating the bread and drinking the fruit of the vine lifts the worshiper into a oneness with the crucified Lord and with fellow believers. The drama, the tangible substance, and the worshiper's ability to participate all help to make it a shared experience with the Savior. And it helps to bring the church into a oneness of fellowship. "For we being many are one bread, and one body: for we are all partakers of that one bread" (I Corinthians 10:17).

It is important to remember that communion is just an enactment of worship. It does not forgive sin, neither do the elements turn miraculously into the literal blood and flesh of Jesus Christ. The doctrine of transubstantiation was developed by the medieval church and was not known to the church of the first century. It is a very sacred act of worship, no more or no less. Nevertheless, Paul told the Corinthians than some were weak, some sickly, and some asleep due to their partaking of the Lord's Supper "unworthily . . . not discerning the Lord's body" (I Corinthians 11:27-29). They had carelessly entered into this sacred enactment in an unworthy manner, not considering its serious nature.

2. *Baptism.* Although baptism was not practiced as a repeatable ceremony, we mention it as an enactment of worship because of its dramatic enactment of the gospel. Baptism was a part of the conversion experience

in the first church (Acts 2:38; 8:12, 16; 10:48; 19:5). All new converts were baptized as a symbolic burial with Jesus (Romans 6:4; Colossians 2:12). We confirm our death to sin by a watery burial, which leads us to spiritual resurrection, the baptism of the Holy Ghost!

Unlike communion, baptism is more than just a worship method. Baptism actually plays a role in the forgiveness of sin. "Repent, and be baptized every one of you in the name of Jesus Christ for the remission of sins" (Acts 2:38). "Arise, and be baptized, and wash away thy sins" (Acts 22:16). Since it is a part of conversion and is involved in the remission of sins, what a time it is to worship! Many have been baptized in the Holy Ghost at their baptism in water due to the nature of this faith-building enactment of worship.

3. *Plays.* Some churches have found this method of worship to be a great expression of faith. Those who participate in the enactment as well as those watching the performance have been inspired to worship when the drama was a presentation that gave glory to the Lord.

Most churches have some type of Christmas program each year to celebrate the birth of the Savior. This can be a great occasion to bring a congregation to a new appreciation of the redemption story. Easter is a good season for plays concerning the resurrection.

A play does not necessarily aid in praise or worship. Some programs are just entertaining, educational, or an exercise in dramatics. Due to the cost, time, and effort required to put a play on, utmost concern should be given to the content and general impact of the play in order to make it induce praise and worship.

4. *Special days.* Religious holidays can be a conve-

nient time to celebrate certain Christian beliefs, although scripturally there are no mandatory religious holidays to the Christian. The Old Testament rituals regarding days and seasons have been done away with. "Let no man therefore judge you in meat, or in drink, or in respect of an holyday, or of the new moon, or of the sabbath days: which are a shadow of things to come; but the body is of Christ" (Colossians 2:16-17).

The early church met on Sunday, the day of Christ's resurrection (Acts 20:7; I Corinthians 16:1-2). Most churches continue this practice today as a matter of tradition and convenience. Since one day is not to be regarded above another, we use the most accepted day as a day of worship. Our day of rest is a perpetual rest in the Holy Ghost, not a particular day of the week (Isaiah 28:11-12; Hebrews 4:1-11).

Other days of the year can be used as a tool to inspire fresh worship. It is doubtful that Jesus was born on December 25; nevertheless, Christmas can be a convenient time to celebrate the gospel story. We can also use such days as Easter, Pentecost, and Thanksgiving as an occasion to add freshness to our praise and worship.

5. *Salutations.* Worshipful greetings have their origin in ancient Israel. When Boaz arrived from Bethlehem he greeted the harvesters with "The LORD be with you," and they called back, "The LORD bless thee" (Ruth 2:4). When Jesus appeared after his resurrection to the disciples His greeting was, "Peace be unto you" (John 20:19).

When we greet another believer it is a great opportunity to offer praise unto the Lord with a hearty "Praise the Lord!" When believers meet it is a joyous occasion, and our joy should include the One who made it all possible.

Those who have directed a service know the jitters they feel having to walk to the pulpit and start things off. The best way to calm these fears and pull the congregation together is to greet them with a praise expression by reading a passage of Scripture, singing a song, or making a statement that praises the Lord.

Notes

[1]Donald O. Bolander, *Instant Quotation Dictionary* (Little Falls, NJ: Career Publishing, 1984), p. 186.

[2]Robert E. Webber, *Worship Old and New* (Grand Rapids, MI: Zondervan Publishing House, 1982), p. 178.

[3]Bolander, p. 207.

[4]*Webster's New Twentieth Century Dictionary of the English Language* unabridged, s.v. "Eucharist."

CHAPTER 8

The Worship Service

*T*he worship service is one of the most effective tools we have to evangelize the sinner. It is also one of the most effective vehicles to edify, unify, and satisfy the believer. And it provides a setting in which to minister collectively unto the Lord in praise and worship.

The worship service is where we meet God face to face. It is a place where we concentrate upon God, reflect upon His blessings, celebrate His triumph, experience His love, and appropriate His benevolent promises. The service is a place where our faith is fortified, our commitment is renewed, our knowledge is expanded, and our spirit is nourished.

The worship service is the showpiece to the world of our love for Jesus Christ and commitment to His body, the church. Every service should be a celebration of Christ's resurrection, pointing the world to the empty tomb. The world must know that we do not come together merely to learn a catechism, to socialize with friends, to do our religious duty, or to dress up. Through the worship service the world can see our consuming devotion to, and faith in, the Lord Jesus Christ as the King of kings and the Lord of lords.

Worship Is Not Preliminary

Most evangelical churches put great importance upon the preaching of God's Word. The platform is the main focus of the service. The lectern is even located in the center of the platform area so that it becomes the central point architecturally. The preaching is usually the latter portion of the service so that it becomes the climax.

Emphasizing the preaching is a wholesome, biblical practice, for "how shall they hear without a preacher?" (Romans 10:14). Our great commission is, "Go ye into all the world, and preach the gospel to every creature" (Mark 16:15). Jesus was both a teacher and a preacher, and He ordained that by this method the lost should hear the gospel and faith be planted in the hearts of men and women (Romans 10:14-17, I Corinthians 1:21). Nevertheless, in our zealous elevation of preaching, we should not minimize the importance of corporate worship, nor ignore the need for preaching to embody and be accompanied by worship.

Can we say that preaching, which ministers to the people, is more important than worship, which ministers unto the Lord? Is ministry to people more important than ministry unto the Lord? Both are important!

Many times the worship service is referred to as the "preliminaries." This word means something that serves as an introduction, going before the main event. It carries with it the connotation of something preparatory or introductory to something greater. When this word is used, the implication is that the purpose of the worship service is merely to get us warmed up for the main event. This concept, whether deliberate or not, can promote a demeaning attitude toward a very important part of the service. Preaching should not be emphasized to the detriment of worship, and vice versa. These two parts of the service will complement each other if both are regarded highly.

A good worship service will prepare the hearts of the congregation for the preaching of the Word of God. Offering praise and thanksgiving opens the door to the spiritual man so that the Word can penetrate and have a lasting effect. And many times preaching will embody worship, lifting the service even higher in worship. The worship service should be like a journey with the preaching bringing us to our destination.

Leading in Worship

Few things are more rewarding or challenging than being a worship leader. Sometimes the congregation will gather with an attitude of expectancy, ready to worship. At other times, they will be haggard, tired, and distracted. The worship leader cannot follow these moods, but he must always exude a constant, positive attitude of worship, which can be an overwhelming task at times.

The worship leader should remember several important points.

1. *He is the leader.* Worshipers assemble together and sit on pews that face the pulpit. They fix their attention on the leader with the anticipation of being led on a spiritual journey. He is their leader, and it is hoped that they are ready to follow. Dwight D. Eisenhower defined

143

leadership as "the art of getting someone else to do something you want done because he wants to do it."[1] Most people come to church to worship even though they may be tired, depressed, carnal, or even despondent. The leader's task is to help them do what they really want to do. A congregation, at times, will appear uninterested. Sometimes they may even resent the leader's prompting them to worship, but when the goal is reached they will be pleased with his urging.

In every congregation there will be people who will not cooperate. Therefore, the leader should concentrate his attention on those who are following. Otherwise he will feel intimidated, or even challenged, by unresponsive individuals. The leader can become preoccupied with the negative individuals, attempt to force participation, and thereby spoil the wholesomeness of the meeting.

People will rarely rise above their leadership. The worship leader cannot blame the congregation if the service goes nowhere. It is the leader's responsibility to lift the congregation into real collective worship. If the service is a flop, the worship leader should take a serious look at the reasons for failure and prayerfully seek ways to improve.

2. *Show, don't tell.* The best way for a leader to motivate people to worship is for he himself to worship. The leader can become so preoccupied with leading that he forgets to worship. When we lead, we must never forget we are worshipers too. As one pastor put it, "We must both preach what we practice and practice what we preach. The great pastoral peril is to succumb to the temptation of being just a coach."[2] When the worship leader truly manifests a love for the Lord, the congregation will

catch his spirit of worship.

3. *Inspire, don't intimidate.* There is nothing that makes me more unhappy than someone trying to make me happy! A worship leader can ruin a service by trying to move a congregation too quickly. People need someone to remind them of how great God is by exhortation, reading of Scripture, a song of praise, or some other method. It would be wonderful if everybody came to the service ready to release themselves in a great expression of praise, but in the real world, that is not the case. Bringing them to that place is the challenge of the leader.

If the leader can help the people to see Jesus, they will worship Him! If the leader becomes angry or frustrated the congregation will shrivel up. From time to time, the people will need a stimulating challenge, but a rebuke should be used only rarely and then in the wise discretion of the pastor and not anyone else. If the congregation is intimidated, they will be distracted from the main goal. People should always be treated with human dignity.

A friend of mine became frustrated with a congregation because of their poor response to his exhortation. In a fit of anger and frustration he told them they reminded him of buzzards perched waiting for something to die. Of course, this statement only made the situation worse. He apologized for the remark later. Probably most leaders, myself included, have made similar blunders. The worship leader's job is one of inspiration, not intimidation.

4. *Don't be a bore.* A congregation can be bored a number of ways. Let us consider them and avoid the pitfalls.

• *Lack of enthusiasm by the leader.* Droning on in a monotonous or unassertive voice will put people to sleep.

• *Repetition of hackneyed cliches.* Over a period of time we can pick up a whole vocabulary of religious verbiage that rolls off people "like water off a duck's back."

• *Lack of direction.* People feel the frustration when the leader is like a man in a dark room fumbling for the door. A leader needs to learn to be sensitive to the leading of the Spirit and to make proper preparation.

• *Telling long stories.* Stories that don't inspire will bore, distract, and deflate the service.

• *Giving an autobiography of the day's activities.*

• *Being unorganized, unprepared, and sloppy.* People are very time conscious in today's fast-paced world. Tuning guitars, playing the scale to find the right key, moving microphones, shifting through notebooks for words to a song, whispering back and forth about the music are a waste of people's time. It also gives the impression that what is being done is really not worth doing well.

• *Excessive talking.* I have been in services where real worship was taking place and the leader interrupted to tell an unrelated story or to expound on a complex spiritual thought. In doing so, he completely stopped the spirit of worship. The leader should not feel compelled to comment on everything. Sometimes less is more! We should let the worshipers worship and the preachers preach! There is a time for all things.

The worship leader is like the apothecaries who prepared the incense for the altar of incense. (See Exodus 30:34-38.) The incense produced a sweet, fresh smell that drifted into the camp of the Israelites. Likewise, the worship leader should strive for sweet freshness. Always being fresh requires effort. Being a good leader in worship is hard work.

The following suggestions are offered to help enhance the worship leader's skills:
- Be prayerful and meditative.
- Scout for new choruses.
- Memorize worshipful passages of Scripture.
- Stay abreast of new methods.
- Be innovative.
- Be a thoughtful planner.
- Be selective with music.
- Learn to empathize with working people and visitors.
- Read books on worship.
- Be observant and learn.
- Learn to be spiritually sensitive.

Good worship services do not just happen. The worship leader plans, organizes, memorizes, and sets goals and themes for the service. Many services are a hodgepodge of themes and subjects, leaving people with their minds scattered. They go home without really retaining anything. A service where the songs, the prayers, the preaching, and the exhortation all blend together on a common theme will make a tremendous spiritual impact.

Often the Holy Ghost blesses when little preparation has been made. Nevertheless, our efforts to find God's leading in advance could help the service be even more effective. Is it more spiritual to find God's will before the service or during the service? Perhaps no one answer will fit all situations. But surely God is not pleased when a lack of preparation is due to a lack of concern or commitment, and He certainly sees through pseudo spirituality that is nothing more than stalling because of lack of preparation.

The Balance of Form and Freedom

Keeping the purpose ahead of the program is the key to a good worship service. And the purpose is to lift people into worship. We can become so preoccupied with the elements of worship that we forget to worship. We can become so paranoid about becoming liturgical that we lose the sanctity of worship in our pursuit of the new and the unpredictable. On the other hand, ritual can become "rutual" leaving people barren of anything spiritual.

We are familiar with the pitfalls of these two extremes. Many churches lean one way or other, either toward starchy formalism or disorganized pandemonium. The goal is to strike a balance between form and freedom.

Paul Anderson wrote, "The issue is not structure of freedom, but Spirit. God has no preference for formless spiritualism or Spiritless formalism—he rejects both. Liberty is where the Spirit is, not where the preacher has thrown away his notes."[3]

The Corinthian church is an example of what happens when "freedom" overrides all form. The Corinthian church was loose and reckless, which resulted in confusion within the church and misunderstanding by outsiders who visited. Paul laid down guidelines for their worship service and for the exercise of the gifts of the Spirit (I Corinthians 12-14).

The complementary interaction between form and freedom has been compared to the roles of priest and prophet in the Old Testament. "The priest is part of the establishment; the prophet points out the weaknesses of the status quo. The priest comforts the afflicted; the prophet afflicts the comfortable. The priest represents the people to God; the prophet represents God to the people."[4] The priest was more comfortable with the scheduled program and therefore more susceptible to complacency. The prophet yearned for the heartthrob of the Spirit and was more susceptible to overzealous recklessness. Together they helped to create a balance.

Churches eventually adopt a pattern in their service arrangement. They may not print a program, but usually regular attenders know what will happen next. This situation is not necessarily bad, for a train on its track is assured of going somewhere. An agenda provides a workable plan that can form the springboard for spontaneity. The agenda is not what puts people to sleep; it is the lack of anointing and freshness that causes somnolence to possess a congregation.

Oddly enough, too much variety and change can be boring. Worship services can become trite and platitudinous if too many tricks and gimmicks are used. They can lose depth and adopt a circus atmosphere. And regardless of how creative we may be, eventually we will run out of novel methods. It is not advantageous to keep people always guessing what will happen next. It might keep the congregation alert with expectancy, but it could distract from real worship. They will be amused and entertained instead of being wooed into the presence of God.

The entire Book of Leviticus concerns instruction to Israel on how to worship. Worship formed the very nucleus of their life, yet these instructions became cold rituals to them at times. More instruction in methods of worship may not be what we need. But a consuming love for the Lord Jesus Christ will inspire worship with or without form.

I heard one pastor say he spent as much time planning a service as he did preparing a sermon. To some, this may seem to be an effort to program the moving of the Spirit. Many pastors call the shots as they go. They are accustomed to "playing it by ear." Their philosophy is, if you do not have a program, the Spirit can have more opportunity to lead. And it is true that if a program is there, the leader will be tempted to stick to it rigidly. But the leader must always be willing to yield the program to the intervention of the Spirit. A well-planned agenda can be anointed by the Holy Ghost to accomplish more in a service than a haphazard groping for direction. John Killinger observed, "I don't think we need to change patterns often. It isn't the format that people grow tired of, it's the routine, insensitive way the format may be handled."[5]

Even the churches that acclaim the most freedom in worship still conform to a schedule in many ways. They have a regular service schedule, and services such as funerals, dramas, communion, weddings, baby dedications, and building dedications are all programed. To be adamantly against all planning of services can rob us of many rich and fulfilling experiences. A planned service can impart a sense of purpose. It can make the participants feel that their best is expected. It can teach the people to work together, and it can make the service more enjoyable for the visitors as well as the regular members.

It is a mistake to think that the success of a service is determined by the volume of noise or the excitement generated. Rather the worship service is a success when the Lord is exalted, the church is edified, and sinners are introduced to the Savior. We should not be satisfied until these three things have been accomplished. But first we must worship, or these objectives will not be achieved. Worship will bring the anointing of God's Spirit.

Music in the Worship Service

Music has an ethereal quality about it that blends well with worship. It is one of the best aids to worship. It has a power to bring people together in unity, wash the mind of foreign thoughts, sensitize the spirit, and bring it to a poise before the Lord. The right music accentuates the words and stimulates the emotion, blending them together and resulting in great spiritual impact. Our music should be the very best we can offer the Lord, for He deserves our best.

Let us consider the following uses of music in the church service.

1. *Before the service.* Many churches sound like a henhouse as the people arrive for service. Of course, the church is a place of fellowship, and it is important not to forbid this vital function of the church. Briefly welcoming visitors is always in order and speaking to fellow members is a good thing. But excessive chatter and socializing can create an atmosphere that is detrimental to the beginning of the service.

Music through the P.A. system can help to drown out some of the noise. The church musicians can play and sing, which will cut down on the visiting. Music before the service helps to set the mood for worship. (In any case, it is hoped that the faithful members will be in the prayer rooms.) An abundance of recorded music is available today that is suitable for such use.

2. *Congregational singing.* Congregational singing brings people together as nothing else will. It affords par-

151

ticipation instead of observation. When selecting hymns and choruses, the song leader should keep in mind that not all of them are equally worshipful. Some songs consist of direct thanksgiving, praise, and worship, while others are about consecration, theology, eschatology, altar appeals, rewards, conversion, testimony, and other subjects. The subject of the song should be prayerfully considered when making selections for a service.

The worship leader should learn by experience the mood of a congregation. Sometimes the people will be ready to praise with a fast, lively number, and sometimes they will need a slow, meditative song to purge their minds and get them in a worshipful mood. Trying to go too fast with the congregation will cause frustration for the leader as well as the congregation. When a leader comes on too strong too quickly a congregation will recoil and throw up a barrier. They will feel intimidated and coerced.

3. *Choruses and hymns.* Both choruses and hymns have their place in the worship service. Choruses tend to be short in length, simple in wording and music, and repetitive of one idea. Choruses can usually be memorized very quickly with the aid of an overhead projector or a chorus book. Hymns are more complex musically, normally have several verses, and are often rich in theology. The hymn in the neatly bound hymnal embodies the more traditional method of expression, whereas the chorus is more contemporary.

The New Testament speaks of three types of songs: "psalms and hymns and spiritual songs" (Ephesians 5:19; Colossians 3:16). Although these terms are difficult to define explicitly in their historical setting, it is apparent

152

that they refer to different types of songs. Donald P. Hustad defined them as follows:

> *Psalms* no doubt included all the psalms and canticles common to Jewish worship—the historic, classical worship expressions known to all Jewish Christians who had grown up hearing them in the temple and the synagogue: songs of praise and thanksgiving to Yahweh, didactic psalms, witness psalms of petition and lament.
>
> *Hymns* were probably new songs that expressed the Christology of the new sect. A number of these hymns appear in Paul's letters, written in the patterns of classical Greek poetry. Like many of the hymns of Martin Luther and Charles Wesley, they were written to express, and thus to teach, Christian doctrine.
>
> The patristic fathers and modern musicologists both agree that *spiritual songs* describe ecstatic singing that was either wordless or had unintelligible words—singing in tongues.[6]

Some churches have thrown out the hymnal and sing only choruses. Other churches are so addicted to the hymnal they cannot enjoy new choruses. The blending of the two will give a balance in worship. Hymns such as "All Hail the Power of Jesus' Name," "Amazing Grace," and "How Great Thou Art" have a powerful worship message. These older songs should not be considered obsolete; they can add richness and depth to a worship service.

Leading a congregation immediately into a chorus at the end of an old hymn can be very effective. The hymn will convey a thorough idea and the chorus will reinforce it. The leader will want to make sure the message of the hymn and chorus agree and that the same key is appropriate.

Worship leaders should always be looking for new choruses to teach the congregation. A chorus book can be compiled to assist visitors in learning them quickly. Projecting the words on an overhead projector will leave the worshipers' hands free to praise. New choruses can add freshness and vivacity to our praise. The psalms repeatedly refer to the "new song" of praise.

4. *Special singing.* Choirs, small groups, and solos are appropriate in worship services, not for entertainment but to inspire the congregation to worship. Gifted singers can be a great blessing if they sing sincerely to praise the Lord and not to display their talent. Their lives should be an example of what they sing about, for talent alone is not enough.

People who do not practice should not be allowed to sing special songs. We are to praise God with the highest praise in effort, quality, and sincerity. Sloppy services with unprepared singers reveal a lack of interest in giving God the best.

The Offering and Worship

Giving is an eternal spiritual principle. "Every man according as he purposeth in his heart, so let him give; not grudgingly, or of necessity: for God loveth a cheerful giver" (II Corinthians 9:7). Offerings provide the worshiper with a great opportunity to give. Unfortunately, the offering many times is a time of strain on the spirit of a service. If receiving the offering quenches the worship, something is wrong. If receiving an offering is a painful interruption, a great worshipful experience is lost.

Reminding the congregation to give thankfully and praying before receiving the offering are helpful ways of making the offering a meaningful experience. During the offering collection, it is also helpful to sing good choruses that proclaim God's bountiful blessings, such as "I Am Blessed," "There's a Joy in Giving," "Count Your Blessings," and "He's Done So Much for Me."

Not just the wealthy worship by giving; everyone can participate. Jesus taught that it is not the amount we give but what we have left that really counts. The poor widow gave two mites, which was less than a penny, but it was all she had. Jesus said, "This poor widow hath cast more in, than all they which have cast into the treasury" (Mark 12:43).

Announcements and Worship

Announcements are like bad medicine; they are hard to swallow but they have to be made. Emphasis put on the purpose of scheduled events will create anticipation and excitement for them. And it is hoped that all the church activities will have a spiritual purpose.

The best time to interject announcements is in the middle of the service, as the intensity of the meeting is building. They allow for a light, perhaps humorous moment and give the congregation a break. At the beginning of the service people's minds are somewhat scattered. At the end of the service they are preparing to have fellowship or return home. In either case, much will not be remembered. Announcement time is also a good time to recognize visitors.

Announcement time can be reduced by using church bulletins and bulletin boards.

Preaching and Worship

Most churches have the bulk of their congregational worship at the first part of the service. This arrangement is effective in preparing people spiritually for the ministry of the Word. The sermon focuses the theme of the service, bringing the loose ends together and concentrating on the individual. The preaching should take the congregation on a spiritual odyssey, leading them to a final climax of destiny. If the sermon takes them nowhere, they will be lost in a verbal wilderness, confused, and misdirected.

The worship service and the preaching are not two distinct and unrelated parts; they should be fused together, complementing one another. Preaching embodies worship, for genuine preaching is a presentation of the gospel of Jesus Christ. Whatever the subject, ultimately the gospel should come forth, and it will inherently exalt the Lord Jesus. Somewhere in the preaching, each individual in the congregation should reach a moment of insight or a sudden flash of intuitive understanding. Warren W. Wiersbe described the preacher's role in this way: "In the preaching of God's Word, the church witnesses both to itself and to the lost world, but this is true only if the preaching is truly an act of worship. If preaching is not an act of worship then the church will end up worshiping the preacher and what he says rather than worshiping God."[7]

During the preaching is not a time to sit back and catch forty winks while the preacher rambles. It should be an engaging occasion of interaction between the congregation and the preacher. I always heard that the best way to get rid of a bad preacher was to sit on the front row and "amen" him vociferously: he would preach himself to death! There is nothing more devastating to a preacher than to make a good point and have a congregation just stare blankly at him as if they were in a comatose condition. It is a very lonely feeling for a preacher to know he has lost his congregation in the quagmire of mental meandering. Many times I have felt sweat running down my neck as I struggled to bring a congregation along with me on a spiritual pilgrimage. Their heel-dragging detachment made me feel as if I were trying to push a freight train alone.

The worshiper must continue to stay poised for praise during the preaching. Many times a service will reach an apex of glorious praise at this stage of the service. If the congregation will continue to feel responsible, and not relinquish everything to the preacher, the services will continue in a deep vein of worship.

The preacher has a great responsibility to the people who have come to worship. Perhaps the following tips will help.

1. Good preparation produces good preaching.

2. If the preacher prays and worships during the preparation of his message, the same will be stimulated in the congregation at the time of delivery.

3. Less is sometimes more. Bored congregations have said it well: "The mind can only absorb what the seat can endure!"; "If you haven't struck oil in thirty minutes, stop boring!" Many good messages have been ruined by long-winded preachers.

4. Lose your identity in the message.

5. Get the anointing of the Holy Spirit. Nothing is more boring than unanointed preaching.

6. When you emphasize everything you emphasize

nothing. Being overly dramatic makes mannerisms seem superfluous.

7. Don't be the hero of all your stories. People love to hear jokes on the preacher. Let them know you are human too.

8. Be organized. Follow some pattern so the congregation can follow your progress.

9. Use language on the level of the congregation.

10. Bring the abstract into focus with real, human examples.

11. Make your objective ministering, not preaching a good sermon.

12. Make abundant use of the Bible, expounding the true meaning of scriptural passages in their context.

13. Surround yourself with good books and use them.

14. Listen frequently to others preach.

15. Become a good worshiper.

A word should be said about the introduction of special speakers. The introduction should be brief and not a biographical rundown. Too much praise can be flattery; even if it is sincere, people will wonder about the intent. Building a speaker up too much will distance him from the audience. They will feel he is so special that he must be very different from them. If he is good, the people will soon find out, if the introducer will let him have the pulpit.

Accessories and Accents to Worship

Jesus established two requirements for worship when He said, "God is a Spirit: and they that worship him must worship him in spirit and in truth" (John 4:24). It is a Christian principle that worship can occur anywhere and under any condition as long as it is done in spirit and in truth. Throughout history Christians have worshiped everywhere—in homes, in catacombs, in prisons, on ships, in automobiles, on airplanes, in fields, in the woods, and in factories. Yet, when possible, it has always been the custom that Christians have a specific place of worship—a church building.

Some may feel that environmental conditions are irrelevant since worship deals with the celestial and not the terrestrial. Discussion of such things as acoustics, lighting, decor, air conditioning, and other such temporal trappings may appear unrelated at first glance. Obviously, these things do not determine true worship, but they can enhance or dampen the intensity of the worshiper. Therefore, the surroundings are not neutral; they can influence the worshiper and also communicate something about the convictions of the people who worship there.

Throughout history worshipers have always had a place of worship. The Israelites had their Tabernacle and Temple and later their synagogues. These places were dedicated unto the Lord as special places of worship (I Kings 8). The early Christian church worshiped in the Temple, in synagogues, in houses, and later in other buildings, as their resources permitted. (See Acts 2:46; 3:1; 18:4; 19:9.) Unfortunately, in the medieval period Christendom became excessively preoccupied with church architecture. Its churches were architectural wonders, but true worship was notably absent.

It is a workable and convenient practice for the contemporary church to meet in church buildings. The benefits of this custom are tremendous. In this regard, let us consider some things that are of extreme importance to insure a good place of worship.

1. *The exterior.* In our society certain modes of architecture convey a building's function. Sometimes the shape and design are for spatial and practical reasons and sometimes they are just traditional. We learn to recognize a warehouse, a restaurant, a bank, a school, a grocery store, and so on by the design of the building. Churches have certain styles of architecture that make them recognizable as a church. There is no advantage in building a church with different style just to be novel. Many aspects of modern church design have been carefully thought out over the years and serve some very practical purposes.

The church should be inviting so that visitors will not be reluctant to come inside. Glass doors and good exterior lighting help a great deal. At one church where I was pastor, the building had wooden doors that were painted a dark brown. A young man who visited told me that one of the hardest things he had ever done was to come past those doors. When he came to our church for the first time, he said, he stood at the door momentarily and almost walked away; then he forced himself to go inside. Truly, the fear of the unknown is one of the greatest human fears. Later, glass doors were installed along with good lighting.

The church's exterior will say a great deal to the community. A neatly cut lawn, well-trimmed shrubbery, swept sidewalks, and fresh paint will do a lot to communicate that the church cares. A good sign advertises the church and makes people feel welcome.

2. *The interior.* The interior should be as roomy as possible to provide worship and fellowship areas. Vaulted

ceilings provide an openness and an upward look. I pastored a small storefront church several years ago that had a beam running through the middle of the sanctuary. The low, eight-foot ceiling and the raised pulpit area put the beam within reach when I raised my hands. I cracked my knuckles on that beam many times before I ever learned my lesson. It was the best we could do at the time, but we had a boxed-in feeling. The height of the eaves of an auditorium should be a minimum of nine feet.

The aisle space is a very important feature of a worshiping church. Five feet should be the minimum width of an aisle, even for a small church. Aisles are not just entrance and exit routes, but they provide a place for people to worship outside their pew. The altar area is also a very needed area in a worshiping church. This area should be as large as affordable. If, due to finances, I had to choose between a choir loft or a spacious altar area, I would choose the altar area.

3. *Colors and furnishings.* Recent studies have indicated that colors affect our attention span and have other psychological effects. Bright colors (reds, oranges, yellows) tend to stimulate, create restlessness, and put the nerves on edge. On the other hand, some police stations now place violent people in pink surroundings to help calm them and make them manageable. Greens and blues tend to be restful also. Dark colors are good environments for sleeping. Ideally, soft, pastel colors are best for walls and perhaps for flooring. Darker colors can be used for curtains, windows, flowers, pews, and trim. A prevailing light, soft color will not put the worshipers to sleep, nor will it put their nerves on edge and make them restless.

The open look is best for worship. I have been in

churches whose platform areas were a maze of railings, narrow, steep stairways, and large, wraparound pulpits. But the church is not a lecture room, nor is it a theater; it is a place of worship. Some churches have taken down the railings and even installed transparent pulpits to give the church a more open look. An open design makes the leader closer to the people, giving him more rapport with the worshipers.

4. *Heating and air conditioning.* People of Third World countries usually do not mind sweating while they worship, but most North Americans are so accustomed to comfort that some think they are bleeding to death if they sweat. Temperature is thus a critical element to consider when building a worship center. I have been in churches that spent all their money on finery and had to install an undersized air unit with no distribution system (air blowing out through grills at one end of the building and only servicing certain areas). Installing an adequate air unit with a good distribution system is a wise investment. Uncomfortable temperatures will distract people from worship.

5. *Lighting.* Good lighting is not only helpful for safe traffic control, but it is also linked to the psyche. When it is possible to control the lighting intensity, brightening a room can add dramatic emphasis and dimming it can help to create a sense of repose and quietness.

Lighting can be used to focus attention. When the choir rises to sing, the lights on them can be brightened; and when they are seated, the lights can be dimmed again. The platform area needs greater lighting because of the activity on it, and to focus attention on the preaching.

We have all sat in churches with hanging globe lights

that burned our eyes like tiny suns on the periphery of our vision. Vaulted ceilings that are high enough can accommodate hanging lights, but caution needs to be taken not to hang lights so that they distract the worshipers. Indirect lighting is very effective in avoiding glare. Experts are available to help determine the correct candlepower and the most appropriate method of lighting a worship center.

6. *Sound system.* The sound system is the final link between the platform and the congregation. In a worshiping church the sound system is important.

When shopping for a sound system it is easy to be misled by salesmen who do not understand the needs of a worshiping church. It is a good idea to invite the sound expert to visit a service before he recommends what equipment to use. Buying the best low-impedance system the church can afford is a good idea. Nothing is more frustrating than an undependable or a poorly designed sound system.

The sound board or sound booth should be located in an area that permits the sound man to hear what the congregation is hearing. Putting it in a side room or balcony could be a mistake. The monitors need to be regulated by someone who can hear them. If a separate control board for the platform area is unaffordable, phones can be used to communicate adjustments. Otherwise, those on the platform will be waving and signaling to the sound booth, causing distractions in the worship service.

Of course, even with the best system that money can buy, if it is not operated correctly the service can be a disaster. Sound experts tell me that everywhere they go they find men in sound booths who are not knowledgeable of their system. Many problems with sound systems stem not from the equipment but from the operators. Some areas have schools for sound operators; also sound stores are usually very helpful in answering questions. A good sound man will never be noticed; a bad one will get lots of attention. That is the dilemma of the man who sits behind the controls in the sound booth (sweat box). God bless him!

7. *Nurseries.* Babies are little, enigmatic creatures who are equipped with an amplified noisemaker of the most discordant kind. These little bundles of humanity can drown out the most fervent preaching. Their sharp, shrill squalling and screeching can cause the most stubborn parent to give them anything, just to get relief from their wailing. Crying babies can be a great distraction. Good, clean nurseries with concerned helpers are important to a good worship service.

As a final word of instruction, the worship leader should dress in a manner that is conducive to worship. By being clean and neat and wearing matching colors he will avoid distracting people from worship. Good pulpit etiquette is also important. It is reassuring to those who bring visitors. It will also help to relax a congregation, so they will not worry about the leader doing or saying something inappropriate.

All the things we have just considered are simply accents to aid in good worship. They are not primary but secondary. They add the final touch to a worship service. God often moves in a great way without them, but having them is helpful to eliminate distractions and facilitate worship.

Notes

[1]Donald O. Bolander, *Instant Quotations Dictionary* (Little Falls, NJ: Career Publishing, 1972), p. 167.

[2]Ben Patterson, "Can Worship Leaders Worship?" *Leadership,* Spring 1986, p. 35.

[3]Paul Anderson, "Balancing Form and Freedom," *Leadership,* Spring 1986, p. 25.

[4]Paul Anderson, "The Feud Between Form and Freedom," *Christianity Today,* May 16, 1986, p. 66.

[5]John Killinger, "Preaching and Worship: The Essential Link," *Leadership,* Spring 1986, pp. 127-128.

[6]Donald P. Hustad, "Let's Not Just Praise the Lord," *Christianity Today,* November 6, 1987.

[7]Warren W. Wiersbe, *Real Worship* (Nashville: Oliver Nelson, 1986), p. 121.

CHAPTER 9

Music and Worship

enry Wadsworth Longfellow said, "Music is the universal language of mankind."[1] We use music to work by, to jog by, to shop by, to calm the baby, for aerobic exercise, for ceremonies, for relaxation, and for entertainment. Music plays an important role from the church to the bar to the parade on Main Street. In this age of technology, our ears are tantalized with more musical pulsations in a week than many ancient kings heard in their lifetimes. Along with this prevalence of music has come a variety of styles also. Musical genre has never been so diverse.

The prevalence and variety of music in the secular world have affected church music. We are seeing some very unusual changes in church music today. The term "gospel music" no longer refers to a style of music but only identifies the purpose of the songs. Contemporary gospel music has adopted all the styles of the secular scene. Paul Baker, in his book entitled *Contemporary Christian Music,* categorizes Christian music in twenty-six different styles, including everything from New Wave to Southern Gospel.[2] Supposedly in an effort to evangelize, contemporary musicians are using every secular genre to appeal to the secular mind.

Pentecostal churches have always used music as a tool of worship. From the days of flat-top guitars, tambourines, accordions, and upright pianos we have now entered a day of powerful electronic equipment, such as electric drums, keyboards, and guitars. Many of our musicians have degrees in music and are leading choirs to sing complicated musical arrangements. This improvement in equipment, education, and talent has brought with it special blessings and challenges. Most of this modern innovation has been good for Christian worship.

Music has always been a subject of controversy. Perhaps the controversy is due in part to its great variety of style, its association with entertainment, its power to affect moods, and its inexplicable nature that defies verbal definition. The vast difference between music today and music in Bible times also makes it an elusive and difficult subject to harness within biblical guidelines.

Even the Gregorian chant, which is the official music of the Roman Catholic Church, has been in controversy through the years as to the authentic rhythm of the original chant.[3] Perhaps the controversy is due, at least in part, to the fact that it is considered sacred music. Biblically, we cannot say that any particular style is "sacred music." But we are not without guidelines. Through the application of biblical principles we can determine what is acceptable and what is not.

The purpose of this chapter is not to solve all controversy concerning style but to emphasize the importance of music in worship and the necessity of balance in its use. We will also take a look at music from a biblical perspective to discuss its origin, its benefits, and its potential for evil.

The Origin of Music

Music is older than humanity. Long before God created humans and the earth as we know it He created an angelic host and gave them special musical ability. For example, when God challenged Job with difficult questions about the creation of the world, one of the questions He asked was, "Who laid the corner stone thereof; when the morning stars sang together, and all the sons of God shouted for joy?" (Job 38:6-7). It is evident that the angels sang and shouted at the creation of the earth, melodiously praising God.

Among the angelic host in the heavenlies were three powerful angels who were given special authority and skills. These high-ranking angels are mentioned on various occasions in the Bible as having special access to the throne of God: Michael, Gabriel, and Lucifer. From scriptural descriptions it appears that Lucifer was a musician in heaven. Perhaps we could call him the minister of music to the angelic host.

Lucifer was described as a very beautiful angel: "Every precious stone was thy covering, the sardius, topaz, and the diamond, the beryl, the onyx, and the jasper, the sapphire, the emerald, and the carbuncle, and gold" (Ezekiel 28:13). He was anointed, beautiful, wise, and he radiated with brightness as he walked up and down in the midst of stones of fire. (See Ezekiel 28:12 17.) Perhaps one of the most outstanding characteristics of

Lucifer was his musical ability. He was not just a player of musical instruments, but his very being, his intrinsic nature, is described in terms of an orchestra of musical instruments.

First of all, Lucifer had rhythm within him, signified by "tabrets" (a drum or tambourine), and he also had ability to make melody, described by "pipes" (a flute) (Ezekiel 28:13). It is interesting to notice that *pipes* is plural, indicating variety of pitch and the ability to blend tones to make harmony. A third type of music connected with Lucifer is mentioned in Isaiah 14:11: "Thy pomp is brought down to the grave, and the noise of thy viols." A "viol" was a stringed instrument such as a harp, lyre, or a psaltery. In short, Lucifer is described in terms of the three basic types of musical instruments: percussion, wind, and string. These are still the three basic categories of musical instruments, with the addition today of the electronic instruments.

The Original Purpose of Music

Of all the activities in the heavenly realm, worship is primary. Every view we get of heaven shows worship around the throne of God, and the angels are the main participators. Isaiah saw seraphim around the throne in heaven saying, "Holy, holy, holy, is the LORD of hosts: the whole earth is full of his glory" (Isaiah 6:3). Revelation 4 and 5 provide grandiose descriptions of worship, including a scene in which multiplied millions of angels (over one hundred million) loudly express the praises of the Lord.[4] The Scriptures state that everything God has created is for Him and for His pleasure, whether in heaven or in earth (Colossians 1:16; Revelation 4:11).

It is safe to assume that Lucifer's musical ability was given to assist in praise and worship around the throne of God. Music is approved by God as a method of worship throughout the Bible, and the Bible reveals no other purpose for music in heaven. Moreover, since Lucifer was described as a most beautiful and lofty created creature in heaven, and worship was the most noble and prevalent activity in heaven, it appears likely that he was heaven's worship leader.

The original purpose of music was worship. If it was the original purpose, it is still God's purpose. Music's supreme function is to assist in worship to God and bring glory to Him. We cannot be so narrow as to say that all music that is not worshipful is wrong, for God wants us to enjoy life and the talents he has given us, but we do need to understand that such music is a concoction of human design. As such, it can become susceptible to many types of human, as well as demonic, pollutants.

The Perversion of Music

Let us picture Lucifer as the worship leader in heaven, leading the angelic host in musical songs of exaltation to the Lord God. Being in the midst of worship, hearing the millions of angelic voices sing in unity, feeling the exhilarating swell of musical tones and blends of harmonic sound, and understanding the great pleasure this worship brought the Lord, Lucifer began to desire worship for himself. He began to lust to sit on the magnificent, sparkling throne. He became exalted in himself because of his great beauty, talent, and position. He said in his heart, "I will ascend into heaven, I will exalt my throne above the stars of God: I will sit also upon the mount of the congregation, in the sides of the north: I will ascend above the heights of the clouds; I will be like the Most High" (Isaiah 14:13-14).

But his rebellion was not successful. "How art thou fallen from heaven, O Lucifer, son of the morning! how art thou cut down to the ground" (Isaiah 14:12). "I beheld Satan as lightning fall from heaven" (Luke 10:18). Lucifer lost his position in heaven and was cast into the earth, taking a third of the angels with him (Revelation 12:4, 9). The Bible does not say that he lost his musical ability, only his position.

Lucifer desires worship, for he came to Jesus in the wilderness and tempted the Lord to bow down to him (Matthew 4:8-10). Since Lucifer continues to struggle for worship, it is reasonable to believe he will use music to achieve his goal and that music can become a human experience that is highly susceptible to demonic manipulation.

The first biblical mention of the human use of music is found in Genesis 4:21, which says that a man named Jubal was the father of those who handle the harp and organ. Jubal was the son of Lamech, who was a descendant of Cain. Both Cain and Lamech were evil, and there is no indication that Jubal used music to worship God. Lamech was the first recorded polygamist and a braggadocious, ruthless murderer. If his family followed his pattern, they were very irreligious and ungodly. Therefore, it is likely that their music was not used to worship God but to sing war songs, braggadocious ballads about their own achievements, and songs of demonic sensuality.

Humans have corrupted music through the ages. The orgy of the Israelites around the golden calf included singing and dancing (Exodus 32:18-19). In warning Israel of the coming judgment, Amos described their debauched music: "That lie upon beds of ivory, and stretch themselves upon their couches, and eat the lambs out of the flock, and the calves out of the midst of the stall; that chant to the sound of the viol, and invent to themselves instruments of musick, like David" (Amos 6:4-5). These people used some of David's godly worship methods for their own fleshly entertainment. Likewise, the idolatrous worship of the Babylonians was accompanied by "all kinds of musick" (Daniel 3:15).

Today, it seems that Satan is using the music scene as never before to propagate his rebellious message. In this age of rock-and-roll, sin is touted through musical styles, demonic graphics, sensual antics, freakish dress, blasphemous lyrics, and decadent lifestyles of the performers. Many youth today are demoralizing themselves by listening to the incessant beat of Lucifer's hypnotic musical intrigue. There is an inherent evil in certain musical styles that accentuates the intended licentiousness.

Today the secular music industry is much larger than the gospel music industry. In 1986 gospel music took 7.5 percent of the recorded music market, a great surge upward from previous years.[5] Even with this increase of interest, it is sad that 92.5 percent of music in America does not, for the most part, glorify God, and much of that percentage glorifies the devil. What is still sadder is that so much gospel music is unscriptural in its lyrics, compromising in its message, and void of any worshipful inspiration. Many musicians are more concerned with marketing than ministry.

173

It is so important to prayerfully and scripturally screen what we listen to. Our churches, our automobiles, and our homes should be free from the subtle intrusion of the devil's music. We cannot partake of everything the gospel music market serves us. Many gospel musicians are young and inexperienced and have only a scant understanding of the Scriptures. They are too young to perceive their music's consequences from a historical point of view. We need to remember that the underlying force behind popular music is its appeal to the masses. In this age of technology the masses are preoccupied with entertainment, pleasure, novelties, and banality. Satan is still using musical perversion to steal worship from the Lord.

Music in Biblical Worship

The first biblical account of humans using music for worship of God is in Exodus 15. After God delivered the Israelites safely across the Red Sea they worshiped God with a great musical celebration. Moses composed a song and the Israelites sang the song together with him. They gave God praise for their victory over the Egyptians. The words of their song contain such beauty, grandeur, and triumph. With great enthusiasm they worshiped their Deliverer! Miriam, Moses' sister, also wrote a song of praise and led the women in dances to the rhythm of the tambourines.

Moses wrote another song recorded in Deuteronomy 32. (See Deuteronomy 31:30.) Again, it is a song acclaiming the perfections of God and His righteous judgment. He taught it to Israel and commanded them to teach it to their children (Deuteronomy 31:19; 22). Therefore Moses is the first person recorded in Scripture to use music as worship, in accordance with God's heavenly paradigm.

Revelation 15:3 brings the "song of Moses" to our attention again. The occasion is near the end of the great tribulation, and the location is the throne of God in heaven. A group of people are singing around the throne and rejoicing because they have "gotten the victory over the beast, and over his image, and over his mark, and over the number of his name" (Revelation 15:2). Significantly, they are singing the "song of Moses" and the "song of the Lamb."

The meaning of this special choral arrangement has various interpretations: (1) The group will consist of both Jews and Gentiles. (2) The song of Moses represents the outward victory of the Lord and the song of the Lamb represents the inward victory. (3) The singers are Jews who have been redeemed by the blood of the Lamb. (4) They are actually singing the same song the Israelites sang on the banks of the Red Sea. Whatever the meaning, it is significant that Moses will have his song sung around the throne of God in heaven! This honor is far greater than receiving the Grammy or the Dove Awards. Moses won't be songwriter of the year, but songwriter of the ages! With harps the saints will sing, "Great and marvellous are thy works, Lord God Almighty; just and true are thy ways, thou King of saints" (Revelation 15:3).

This great honor given to Moses illustrates the appreciation God has for musicians who use their talent to exalt Him in worship. Much of the gospel music today is horizontal in its ministry. In other words, it is directed to people in and out of the church. But the original purpose of music was vertical—offerings of words and melody directly to the Lord in appreciation of His greatness. Strange things are happening in the gospel music world as a result of musicians trying to appeal to the sinner. Music can certainly be used in evangelism. Nevertheless, if great caution is not used, the world will salt the church instead of the church salting the world.

Moses' use of music to worship God is the first recorded instance in the Bible of earthly worship music, but it certainly is not the last. Deborah and Barak rejoiced in worship with a song of victory after defeating Sisera and his nine hundred chariots of iron. Sisera had oppressed Israel for twenty years, and their celebration of victory included music as worship (Judges 5).

The next great example of someone who worshiped with music was King David. A talented musician and a devoted worshiper, David put music and worship together to create a synergistic duo of dynamic expression. He wrote many songs in the great hymnbook of Israel called the Psalms, introduced all types of musical instruments in worship, appointed choirs and music directors, and organized continual praise and worship around the ark of the covenant at Mt. Zion.

Solomon followed David's example and became a prolific songwriter (1,005 songs according to I Kings 4:32). He retained all the different types of musical instruments David had made, along with the choirs of singers (II Chronicles 7:6).

Jehoshaphat and the army of Judah went to battle once with singers leading in the attack, singing worship songs unto the Lord. After God ambushed the enemy armies and caused them to destroy themselves, the people of Judah returned to Jerusalem and celebrated a miraculous victory "with psalteries and harps and trumpets unto the house of the LORD" (II Chronicles 20:28). Hezekiah's revival included musical worship around the Temple (II Chronicles 29:17-30). Always with restoration and revival Israel used music to celebrate and worship (Ezra 3:10; Nehemiah 12:27).

The New Testament is not as replete with vivid examples. Nevertheless, enough evidence is there to prove that music was definitely a part of New Testament worship. With such a rich Jewish background, Christianity certainly continued in this musical heritage. Let us briefly discuss the evidence for music in the early church.

Singing

Singing as worship was a common practice of Jesus and His disciples, as well as the New Testament church. Jesus sang a hymn with His disciples at the Last Supper just before leaving to go to the Mount of Olives (Matthew 26:30). The anointed, worshipful singing of Paul and Silas preceded the earthquake that God used to shake the Philippian jail at midnight (Acts 16:25). Paul admonished the church to sing psalms, hymns, and spiritual songs (Ephesians 5:19; Colossians 3:16). And Hebrews 2:12 says, "In the midst of the church will I sing praise unto thee." (See also I Corinthians 14:15; James 5:13.)

Although singing in New Testament times was far less complex than our group singing today, it was still a joint chorus of unified expression. Through the years music has evolved to a place of sophistication. Musicians today are concerned with blend, intonation, tone color, style, rhythmic integrity, and so on, which make modern music far more complicated than the songs of centuries ago. Nevertheless, singing was part of New Testament worship, lifting the spirit in praise and worship.

Singing with Musical Instruments

Some churches today forbid the use of musical instruments in the worship service on the ground that the New Testament does not explicitly tell us to use them. They believe that God does not like musical instruments in worship.[6] But if God did not want the use of musical instruments in worship, why did He not say so in His Word? We have a rich heritage of musical instruments the Old Testament, and there is an abundance of praise with musical instruments in heaven. There is no biblical commandment forbidding the use of musical instruments in worship. It would be a strange thing if God enjoyed all the talents of people as praise—such as singing, writing, painting, building, verbal expression—with the exception of playing musical instruments.

The Greek word *psallo* is used four times in the New Testament, and in every case it is connected with praise. The *KJV* translates it as "making melody" in Ephesians 5:19 and as "sing" in Romans 15:9; I Corinthians 14:15; and James 5:13. The primary meaning of this word is "to twitch, twang, to play a stringed instrument with the fingers."[7] If the writers had intended that praise not be accompanied with music they could have used the word *ado,* which means just to sing.[8]

Paul used brass, cymbals, pipes, harps, and trumpets as illustrations when teaching the Corinthian church about the virtue of love and the proper use of spiritual gifts (I Corinthians 13:1; 14:7-8). It is certain from these passages that the church was familiar with musical instruments. He also admonished the church to sing psalms (Ephesians 5:19; Colossians 3:16), and many of the psalms in the Book of Psalms, which is the inspired Word of God, command us to praise God with musical instruments. It would be ironic to sing these commands while teaching that God does not want us to obey them.

Music in Heaven

God will ultimately restore pristine holiness to music and destroy every corrupted sound. God will purge the earth during the great tribulation, and with His great destruction of evil He will also put an end to polluted earthly music. Of Babylon it is said, "The voice of harpers, and musicians, and of pipers, and trumpeters, shall be heard no more at all in thee" (Revelation 18:22). Heaven will resound with musical tones of worship around the throne.

The chief instrument described in heaven is the harp. The harp was always symbolic of joy in Israel. When there was no joy there was no use of harps. During the Babylonian captivity, the captives hung their harps upon the willows, signifying their loss of joy (Psalm 137:2). The harp was used as a wide-range, full-scale instrument much like the piano today.

The twenty-four elders around the throne, who represent the redeemed church, are pictured as worshiping with harps (Revelation 5:8). The song of victory of the 144,000 who overcome the Antichrist in the tribulation is represented by the sound of harps emanating from heaven (Revelation 14:2). Then Revelation 15:2 says that at the throne of God they are given the harps of God to play as they sing of Moses and of the Lamb.

179

This great restoration of music is depicted in Revelation 4 and 5. There the activity of heaven is focused around a beautiful throne sitting on a pavement of crystal with an emerald rainbow round about it. One sits upon the throne, and His appearance is like jasper and sardine stone. The saints are dressed in white robes with crowns on their heads. They have golden bowls of incense in one hand, which are their prayers, and in the other hand harps. They fall before the throne, cast their crowns before the Lord, and begin to sing the song of redemption. All the host of heaven joins in the song until the swells of triumphant worship fill the universe and every creature in the cosmos is compelled to sing along and magnify the Lamb of God. What a day that will be! Thousands of harps and millions of voices will harmoniously serenade this coronation of the King of kings and Lord of lords.

Worldly music will be silenced forever. The devil's music will turn to the moans and screams of the damned as his kingdom tumbles into anarchy at that great day of the Lord. Ultimately, Satan will be stripped of all his glory and will be cast into the lake of fire forever. His music will stop as his torment consumes him (Revelation 20:1-10). Worldly music, with all its sensationalism, overkill, gimmicks, vulgarity, and extravagance will never be heard again! Only the song of the redeemed ones will be heard: "Thou art worthy . . . thou wast slain, and hast redeemed us to God by thy blood out of every kindred, and tongue, and people, and nation. . . . Worthy is the Lamb that was slain to receive power, and riches, and wisdom, and strength, and honour, and glory, and blessing. . . . Blessing, and honour, and glory, and power, be

unto him that sitteth upon the throne, and unto the Lamb
for ever and ever" (Revelation 5:9-13).

Music as an Accessory to Worship

It is impossible to measure the awesome power music
has on the human mind and emotions. Words alone can
have a great impact, but with the right music the words
can be indelibly branded upon the mind. Teachers use
music to teach the ABC's; nations use music to inspire
patriotism; advertisers use music to imprint their message
on our minds; the social protesters of the '60s used music
to express their anger and rebellion against society; the
civil rights movement marched to the theme "We Shall
Overcome."

If we took all music away from worship we would
drastically hamper our ability to express the sentiments
of the heart. We would greatly hinder our reaching out
to God for communion with Him, for music generates
elusive emotions that help lift the will to harmonize the
human spirit with God's Spirit. Music has a quality about
it that is closely associated with the wonder and the
mystery of God.

Jehoshaphat, the king of Judah, and Jehoram, the
king of Israel, once united their forces to battle against
Moab. They did not consult the Lord about their enter-
prise but confidently marched forth to battle. After they
had traveled seven days they discovered that they had
traveled in a circle and were stranded in the wilderness
with no water. At this point they decided to inquire of
the Lord. They called upon Elisha to prophesy in the midst
of this dilemma. Before he prophesied he requested a
minstrel to play. When the minstrel played, the Spirit of

181

the Lord came upon Elisha, and he prophesied, giving direction to the armies of Israel and Judah (II Kings 3:15). Music assisted the prophet in lifting him above the despair of the circumstances, and perhaps soothed his frustration with the careless kings, so he could hear from God.

Clearly, music is an aid to worship. Let us discuss four reasons why.

1. *Music portrays the wonder of God.* Music has a natural ambiguity and abstractness. What makes music alive and vital is difficult to assess and understand. Certain tones and blends of sound affect our emotions and moods in mysterious ways, lifting us at times into a feeling of awe and wonder. In this way, music helps to harmonize our spirit with the transcendence of God.

2. *Music symbolically explores the mysteries of life.* Calvin Johansson, in his book *Music and Ministry: A Biblical Counterpoint,* explained, "Music explores the mysteries of the essence of life: tension and release, struggle and conquest, movement and stillness, sound and silence, growth and decline, affirmation and rejection, life and death, and so on. They are dealt with symbolically rather than factually."[9] This portrayal of life in sound gives motion to the spirit and transports us into a spiritual, heavenly realm.

3. *Music provides creative, artistic expression.* We are created in the image and the likeness of God, which indicates that we have a degree of creative ability. We are limited in our creative skills in that we can only assimilate and reorganize what God has already created. Music is the blending together of sounds in a harmonious way, giving back to God an offering we call art. Those who are gifted in music have an opportunity to be wise

stewards of their God-given talent and develop it as an expression of worship.

4. *Music reflects God's divine order.* As chapter 10 will discuss, there is a prevailing order and consistency in the universe as well as in God's spiritual kingdom. Order is the characteristic that distinguishes music from random noise. The contrast between an orchestra tuning up and the same orchestra playing a musical piece is tremendous. The symmetry of rhythm, tone, melody, harmony, and timbre blend together to align with God's nature as an artistic accompaniment.

Pitfalls of Music

As beneficial as music is in aiding worship, there are still dangers or pitfalls to consider. As with all of our efforts to please God, music in worship must be used according to biblical guidelines. Aside from worldly music with all its decadence, there are pitfalls associated with music in the church service.

1. *The entertainment syndrome.* Perhaps no society in history has ever spent so much time and money solely for the sake of entertainment as our society does today. Technology has made work easier and faster while providing more leisure time than ever before. Entertainment has become one of the largest industries in America, providing giant amusement parks, a vast array of sporting events, continuous television programming, movie theaters, video stores, recreational parks, fashionable nightclubs, musical concerts of every kind, exotic restaurants, and every imaginable amusement to titillate the human craving for pleasure.

This intoxication with pleasure can also inebriate the

church and cause us to think that entertainment is part of our responsibility to society. We must admit that there is a certain amount of entertainment in our preaching, teaching, and music. Nevertheless, entertainment should never become a primary objective. We should strive to make all our activity interesting and captivating, and sometimes it may even be amusing. Our church services should not be boring routines lacking in excitement. We should pursue excellence in our programs and activities so as to attract people and to let them know we are serious about God and them. But entertainment must only be a peripheral by-product of our attempts to capture the minds and emotions of people. Entertainment is only appropriate when it leads people to our chief objective, which is to preach the gospel and exalt the Lord Jesus Christ.

True worship music is sacred music. It does not merely amuse and entertain the crowd, but it lifts the spirit and extols the greatness of God. Musicians who entertain draw attention to themselves by wearing glamorous clothing, using elaborate staging, assuming a superficial and showy demeanor, and performing music that emphasizes style and talent rather than message.

2. *Excessive use of music.* Music is just a small part of the whole picture when it comes to worship. We can worship without music. Music is only a supporting aid to help add impact to words of praise and worship. It would be counterproductive to become too dependent upon music to produce worship.

Some churches have become concert halls where music dominates. But remembering a few catchy poetic lines will not bring us victory when the devil assaults us.

In time of temptation we cannot instantly retrieve the euphoric emotional feeling we experienced during the great swells of organ music. Spiritual warfare is not that simple! A song might be of great help at times, but life is complex and varied. Christians need frequent instruction from the Word of God in order to fight the adversary. The sword of the Spirit, which is the Word of God, is the only offensive weapon we have (Ephesians 6:17). We need large doses of preaching and teaching to establish and preserve our footing spiritually. When we come together we should sing songs, shout for joy, clap, rejoice, testify, preach, teach, and have fellowship with music or without music. Music should never control our worship; our worship should control our music.

3. *Ego conflicts.* I talked to a man one time who stopped going to church because someone unplugged his guitar. And what is worse than not having a good pianist? Having two! The music department is the war department in some churches. The pastor must have the wisdom of Solomon and the patience of Job to handle the jealousy, competitiveness, and the swelled egos of some musically talented people.

Tim LaHaye, elaborating on the temperament theory of Hippocrates, has divided people into four basic temperaments: sanguine, choleric, phlegmatic, and melancholy.[10] It is interesting that he places the artist and musician in the melancholy temperament. A person with this temperament has many good qualities: typically he is loyal, idealistic, sensitive, self-sacrificing, self-disciplined, gifted, and a perfectionist. Nevertheless, he also tends to have some negative traits that make him difficult to get along with: he can be moody, negative, critical, self-

185

centered, touchy, revengeful, and unsociable. Of course, not all musicians can be classified as melancholic, and they do not necessarily have these traits. Moreover, a person can work successfully to improve these faults, particularly through the power of the Holy Spirit.

Church musicians and singers should strive hard to avoid competitiveness with each other. They should avoid being possessive of church musical instruments and positions. Effort should be made to suppress any egotistical desire for recognition and to let God be magnified through their talent. Being submissive to those in authority is imperative in order to avoid confusion and be obedient to biblical guidelines.

4. *Worldliness.* The church is to be the salt of the earth and the light of the world (Matthew 5:13-14). We are to be the models of how to live the good life, heavenly ambassadors, and living epistles read of people (II Corinthians 3:3; 5:20). God's people have always been different from their contemporaries, for God expects His people to set their own course based on the divine principles of God's Word. For example, the prophet Amos became a plumbline to the generation of his day (Amos 7:7-8). God honored the words of the prophets, and their words judged the generation in which they were given.

There is a great danger of the church abdicating this responsibility in the area of music. A missionary told me that after four years of living out of the United States he saw many changes when he returned. His greatest shock was the change in music. For some reason, church people often feel a compulsion to parrot the world's music and abandon their own. Musical styles are so elusive and abstract that it is difficult to be specific in this area, but let us try.

186

There is a music style that attempts to copy current popular music. It has heavy bass, a strong up-and-down beat, very little melody, rapid and high-pitched guitar licks, sustained high-frequency sounds, and voices that articulate words in a guttural, chantlike fashion. Some of these elements exist in various styles, but the combination of them creates a unique style that we did not inherit from our spiritual forefathers; rather, it comes directly from the current rock music scene. As already stated, there is no such thing as a sacred style in music. Nevertheless some styles, such as the one just described, do not inspire worship, regardless of the quality of the words, and therefore should not be used. Such music is wrong because it elicits primarily a physical, sensual response and communicates to the spirit feelings of confusion, discord, rebellion, violence, or frustration.

I have sat through many services where a spirit of worship was stymied by a song that had lovely words but discordant music. Without being technical, here are two suggestions to help the worship leader avoid such music. First, he should observe the styles of music that inspire and the styles that stagnate. Second, he should be aware that music that induces dancing is not always music that induces worship. Dancing before the Lord is praise, but dancing to rhythm is sensuality.

We can become so preoccupied with riding the razor's edge of current styles and trends that our worship becomes polluted with worldliness. Contemporary music is not necessarily good music. The worldly religious musician looks with disdain on the more traditional gospel music, not appreciating its inspiring effects on the worshiper. He does not care that his music has little or no positive spiritual effect; he only wants to be contem-

187

porary. This is a pitfall we must avoid. Our purposes for using music in worship should be to focus attention upon God and glorify Him, bring conviction to the lost, and unify believers in an experience of praise and spiritual worship.

Notes

[1]Donald O. Bolander, *Instant Quotation Dictionary* (Little Falls, NJ: Career Publishing, 1969), p. 186.

[2]Paul Baker, *Contemporary Christian Music* (Westchester, IL: Crossway Books, 1985) pp. 242-57.

[3]John Rayburn, *Gregorian Chant: A History of the Controversy Concerning Its Rhythm,* (Westport, CT: Greenwood Press, 1964), p. xi.

[4]In Revelation 5:11 angels are numbered at 10,000 times 10,000, which equals 100,000,000. In addition there are 1,000s of 1,000s, which would be at least 2,000 times 2,000, or 4,000,000. This would be a total of 104,000,000 angels. Also the Greek word *murioi,* which means myriads, is used here. A myriad means 10,000, or an indefinite number.

[5]Edna Gundersen, "Singing the Praises of Gospel," *USA Weekend* April 17-19, 1987, p. 4.

[6]See Alvin Jennings, *Traditions of Men Versus the Word of God* (Fort Worth, TX: Bible Publications, 1973), p. 141.

[7]W. E. Vine, *Vine's Expository Dictionary of New Testament Words* (McLean, VA: MacDonald Publishing Company), p. 740.

[8]James Strong, *Strong's Exhaustive Concordance of the Bible* (McLean, VA: MacDonald Publishing Company).

[9]Calvin M. Johansson, *Music and Ministry: A Biblical Counterpoint* (Peabody, MA: Hendrickson Publishers, 1984), p. 97.

[10]Tim LaHaye, *Understanding the Male Temperament* (Old Tappan, NJ: Fleming H. Revell Company, 1977), p. 56.

CHAPTER 10

Maintaining Order in Worship

Let all things be done decently and in order
(I Corinthians 14:40).

We observe in our surroundings that everything is in a constant state of flux. God's natural creation is in a process of dying, growing, moving, diminishing, and increasing, which results in a constantly changing world. And our universe is filled with great variety. Paradoxically, in spite of this constant change and variety there is a prevailing order to it all. God's control of everything brings a balance to nature. His constant laws are at work invisibly to maintain order and consistency.

The scientist can measure time to the fraction of a second by the order of the earth's movements around the sun. The botanist can predict the outcome of cross-pollination of plant life by using consistent genetic laws.

Engineers design airplanes that fly and ships that float by using dependable laws of nature that are a result of God's natural order.

We must conclude that although God's creation is filled with diversity and continual change it is at the same time controlled by divine order. God is deliberate in what He does. He does not make random decisions based on whims and moods. He never oscillates, is doubleminded, or changes His rules because of moodiness. There is a prevailing coherence and consistency in the midst of all the change and variety.

God has allowed us great variety in worship: verbal expression, physical display, musical instruments, singing, and even silence. He has ordained worship for all cultures, all time periods, all generations, and all personalities. Even though worship is a free expression and should be done with enthusiastic vigor, there are parameters of control. There is a prevailing divine order in worship based on principles of God's Word. Even though worship is a free expression from the heart, it still must be controlled by divine authority.

There are many examples of order in the Bible.

1. *Order in heaven.* Lucifer's rebellion put him in conflict with God's divine order in heaven. As a result, he was expelled along with his entourage of disorderly angels (Isaiah 14:12-15; Ezekiel 28:13-19). This expulsion indicates God's resolve to maintain order. Every view of heaven in God's Word shows order. (See Isaiah 6; Revelation 4; 5; 15; 21.)

2. *Order in the Old Testament.* Many examples can be cited to illustrate God's divine order. The law was a complete system of rules of order: priesthood, Tabernacle

layout, order of the Israelite camp, dietary laws, ceremonial laws, civil laws, and so on. Everything the Israelites did was controlled by divine order.

When God gave Israel special deliverance from their enemies He gave order to their battle plan. The walls of Jericho fell after very explicit obedience to God's strange, but orderly, instructions. Gideon defeated the Midianites with three hundred men whose only weapons were trumpets, pitchers, lamps, and their vocal cords (Judges 7). Their victory was a result of their harmony with and obedience to God's battle strategy.

3. *Order in the home.* The family should be a holy institution of order, love, and divine authority. Scripturally, order in the home is structured as follows: "The head of every man is Christ; and the head of the woman is the man" (I Corinthians 11:3). "Children, obey your parents in the Lord: for this is right. Honour thy father and mother" (Ephesians 6:1-2). A home that does not have order under Jesus Christ is an unhappy, confused, and misdirected home.

4. *Order in the church.* The apostle Paul compared the church to a human body (I Corinthians 12:12-31). Each person in the church should function as a particular member of the body, of which Christ is the head. No illustration could show more unity than the human body. There are a variety of gifts and a diversity of operations, yet all of them come from the same Spirit. Their purpose is to exhort, edify, and comfort the church. Even though a person receives spiritual gifts as a channel of God, he is still subject to the order of God's Word. That is, he is not to "use God," he is to be used by God. Operating in the spiritual realm does not mean we are lifted into a new

191

dimension that releases us from the laws of divine order.

God has put a variety of ministries and gifts in the church (I Corinthians 12:28; Ephesians 4:11). These ministries and gifts are to function together as a unit. They should function in an orderly fashion for the purpose of edifying the body of Christ. Individually, we are specialized, and together we are organized.

The balance of controlled order and freedom of expression is a paradox. Adherence to strict rules of order without a spirit of obedience and understanding is legalism. Order becomes dead formalism when there is a loss of spontaneity and feeling. Focusing on rules of order with a tunnel vision produces a lopsided perspective of things. On the other hand, to throw away the rules of order would put us in the other ditch. An uncontrolled service that is without rules can deteriorate into a wild, disoriented clamor. It is dangerous to think that because our activity is anointed there are no limits or restraints.

This chapter will discuss the maintaining of order in worship. We will deal primarily with the church service itself since it is where most problems can occur. This subject can be delicate, for too much instruction and caution about order and worship etiquette can cause us to become self-conscious. A preoccupation with mannerisms and order will stymie our worship. We must not make formalism a virtue, nor should we restrict the variety of expression given us in the Word of God. Our objective should be to become better worshipers.

The following principles will provide a guide as we strive to maintain order in our worship and at the same time allow the Holy Spirit to lead.

Authority of the Worship Leader

Obey them that have the rule over you, and submit yourselves: for they watch for your souls, as they that must give account, that they may do it with joy, and not with grief: for that is unprofitable for you (Hebrews 13:17).

God has invested the worship leader with authority to match his responsibility. He is responsible for the progress of the service, and his authority must be respected. God will not inspire a person to do anything against the authority that He ordains.

There are two opposing spiritual forces in our universe: God's authority and satanic rebellion. All things were created and are maintained by God's divine authority. "Thy throne, O God, is for ever and ever: a sceptre of righteousness is the sceptre of thy kingdom" (Hebrews 1:8). "For thine is the kingdom, and the power, and the glory, for ever. Amen" (Matthew 6:13). Since God is the authority of this universe we must submit ourselves to Him in a spirit of obedience. If we have that spirit of obedience we will also submit to God's delegated authority.

I have two children. Many times I will send one with a message to the other. They are sent as my representative with a message from me. If I send my daughter to tell my son to come in out of the rain and he does not obey, then he has disobeyed me. In that situation my daughter represents me as a delegated authority. Some people say they report only to God. They presumptuously think they and the Lord are private buddies and no one else is involved in their relationship. Such thinking is unscriptural. Since we are a body, every Christian is responsible to the other members (I Corinthians 12). As we grow spiritually we will think more collectively and less individually.

193

We are to respect and honor all authority. All those in authority are ministers of God within the scope of their delegated work (Romans 13:1-7). If we are to submit to the supervisor at the job, the policeman on the streets, the judge in the courtroom, and the teacher in the classroom, how much more are we to submit to the person in charge of the worship service!

Satan's rebellion against God's authority terminated his angelic position and responsibilities in heaven. Even though Saul did something religious by offering a sacrifice, it still displeased God because it was tainted with rebellion. Samuel rebuked him for it, saying, "To obey is better than sacrifice, and to hearken than the fat of rams. For rebellion is as the sin of witchcraft, and stubbornness is as iniquity and idolatry" (I Samuel 15:22-23).

Rebellion is perhaps the worst sin, because it is more than specific conduct or an act of wickedness; it is an attitude that will pervade a person's life. A rebellious person will encounter many problems in Christian service. His rebellious spirit will pollute everything he attempts to do for God.

When the Lord sent out seventy disciples to minister among the people, He gave them power to heal the sick, cast out devils, and preach the kingdom of God. He also gave them authority, delegated authority. Jesus told them, "He that heareth you heareth me; and he that despiseth you despiseth me; and he that despiseth me despiseth him that sent me" (Luke 10:16). When someone ignores or shows disrespect for the leadership in a worship service, he manifests a spirit of rebellion, not against that person but against God.

It is important to remember that, regardless of the

intensity of our experience in worship, we never become exempt from the authority of the worship leader. The same truth also applies to the use of spiritual gifts. We can become so caught up with our own personal experience that we become detached from what the Holy Spirit is doing for the church collectively. We must strive to synchronize with the spirit of the service and its leadership.

The gifts of the Spirit are discussed in I Corinthians 12-14, in which great emphasis is placed upon the church as a body. This metaphoric illustration indicates the necessity of order and harmony among the members, which are necessary for the gifts to edify the church. An important principle is, "The spirit of the prophets are subject to the prophets. For God is not the author of confusion" (I Corinthians 14:32-33). In other words, those who are anointed or inspired have the responsibility to use their gifts in an appropriate, harmonious, beneficial way.

If there is a problem, it is not the Holy Spirit's fault. Confusion is always the result of the human vehicle. The Spirit of God will never create a discordant atmosphere. Even the prophets are subject to each other and to the assembly. "Let the prophets speak two or three, and let the other judge" (I Corinthians 14:29).

A maverick, independent attitude will hinder our ability to worship. If we yield to the Holy Ghost and are submissive to godly leaders we will not have to worry about getting out of order. When worshiping alone we can be oblivious to our surroundings, but when worshiping with a group, proper guidelines need to be observed so that the group is edified.

Let us consider several problem areas concerning order in worship. These points are offered sincerely for the purpose of enhancing our worship unto the Lord.

Is Being Wild a Virtue?

I have heard worship leaders say, as they exhorted the congregation to liven up their worship, "The wilder it is the better I like it!" or "Let's be wild with our worship tonight!" I think I know what they meant; nevertheless, is *wild* a good choice of words?

Webster's New Twentieth Century Dictionary gives a number of meanings for the word *wild*. A sampling indicates that the word does not adequately describe real worship: "savage; uncivilized; primitive; immoral; violent; angered; crazed; not submitting to control; rash; in a state of disorder." Intentions are more important than words; nevertheless, words are our means of communication. Using the word *wild* in the sense just given would mean that worship is a time of uncontrolled, savage behavior in which people do abnormal things, no holds are barred, and people go crazy. Thus, *wild* might be a word to describe what worship is not.

According to *Webster's Dictionary,* the word *berserk* comes from the old Norse legends. Warriors would chant war songs until they worked themselves into a frenzy called the "berserker rage." Then they would fearlessly attack hapless villages like raging savages. A congregation can be pumped up to a climax of intense emotion in a similar way. People may become greatly excited about what will happen in the service or over some truth from God's Word. There may be a prevailing anticipation of something great about to happen. But real praise and worship always concentrates on Jesus Christ, glorifying His essence and not the accompanying features of His kingdom.

We can get so excited about what we are going to

do that we forget to do it! I have seen people have great emotional experiences as a result of excitement about what the church could accomplish, leave the service, and do nothing to see the thing come to pass. If we are not careful we will be like the train conductor who loved to blow the whistle: he blew the whistle so much that he ran out of steam to power the engines. Similarly, I once heard a pastor scold his church by telling them they had a good engine but their transmission was messed up. They had lots of excitement and power, but they were not moving anything.

Referring again to the word *wild, Webster's Dictionary* also says it can mean "strong emotion or mental excitement; eager or enthusiastic," and this meaning is acceptable. Our worship and praise should be enthusiastic, intense, with desire, uninhibited, free, ecstatic, fervent, and ardent. But our worship should never be imprudent, reckless, disorderly, confused, crazed, uncontrolled, or violent.

Attention Seekers

In churches of any significant size, there will always be the personality type that loves attention. Some people are not satisfied until they are in the front and center with all eyes upon them. Children and mentally ill individuals may be in this group.

Apostolic worship allows much freedom of expression. Most congregations are urged to express physical display in worship. Due to the general mood of most apostolic services, an attention seeker can have a heyday.

Attention seeking is out of order in a worship service. A person should not demonstrate to please, impress, or gain the attention of the worship leader or the members of the congregation. Some who fall into this category think that demonstrating in some physical fashion is proof of their spirituality. Nothing could be further from the truth. Jesus said, "By their fruits ye shall know them" (Matthew 7:20). The real evidence of spirituality is spiritual fruit, Christian character, and godly conduct.

To some, it is a very humbling thing to dance, leap, or shout. It requires a great crucifixion of the flesh to step out and worship in such a manner. On the other hand, to some such expressions come very easily, and their freedom can even develop into spiritual pride. But there must be humility in our worship. John the Baptist said it well, "He must increase, but I must decrease" (John 3:30). Nothing we do should distract from the glory that only God deserves.

Extreme demonstrations are questionable. One night at prayer meeting a young man in the church where I was pastor suddenly shouted, leaped into the air, and did a complete back somersault, without hands, and landed on his feet. Needless to say, we were all very amused at such a feat and impressed with his gymnastic skills. It got him much attention and got the Lord none. Running the backs of the pews, cartwheels, somersaults, and other acrobatic feats are very impressive, but we must ask, Impressive to whom? Our expressions should draw attention to God alone.

The Lord is so great that "no flesh should glory in his presence" (I Corinthians 1:29). Excessive physical expression can become a superfluous competitive game. Worship is too sacred for ostentatious exhibition. Caution should be taken to avoid letting a worship service deteriorate into a parade of the flesh. We should wonder only at God. "Blessed be the LORD God, the God of Israel, who only doeth wondrous things. And blessed be his glorious name for ever: and let the whole earth be filled with His glory; Amen, and Amen" (Psalm 72:18-19).

Considering the Visitor

As I worked at my desk one day, I overheard a conversation in the next cubicle that caught my attention. A fellow worker was describing a visit to a Pentecostal church. He began telling about the scene in a very carnal, yet sincere way. His description went something like this: "The hand clapping and singing got louder and louder, when suddenly a lady began running around the church! When the preacher saw her, he leaped from the pulpit and chased her all the way around the building!" In the eyes of this bewildered visitor, the preacher was chasing the lady.

We need God's wisdom in knowing where to draw the line between caring and not caring what people think. Probably most of us care too much what visitors think. Considering what visitors may think is a valid concern, for Romans 14:16 instructs us not to let our good be spoken of as evil. (See also I Corinthians 14:23; II Corinthians 8:21.) Nevertheless, caring too much can create inhibitions in our worship in the presence of visitors. To be good worshipers we must abandon our pride and yield ourselves to the Spirit. The key is to strive for balance between caring and not caring.

The Bible has given us a whole array of ways to worship, including dancing, leaping, hand clapping, lifting of hands, shouting, and singing. We should be able to praise the Lord in a true and wholesome way using these biblical methods. If visitors do not understand these methods, we have God's Word to back us up. On the other hand, we should be very careful about engaging in things that cannot be biblically supported.

When our expressions are scripturally supported we can easily explain our behavior to the outsider and so should not feel inhibited. If our activity is unscriptural, we could have a problem. In sum, a physical expression is appropriate as long as it is done sincerely, is in harmony with the spirit of the service, and can be supported scripturally.

Most modern Christian denominations are so removed from the apostolic pattern that they think true biblical worship is strange and excessive. If this is the feeling of the denominational world, then unchurched people must really have reservations about true worship. Therefore, some criticism is inevitable, and misunderstandings will occur even when we are truly worshiping the Lord. But to consider the outsider is not to quench the Spirit. We should avoid anything that would be questionable biblically. Being deliberately strange and abnormal just to magnify our uniqueness does not give us any advantage.

Empathizing with visitors can add freshness to our worship. Putting ourselves in their place will cause us to think sincerely about what we are doing instead of just routinely going through a formality. We need to challenge ourselves to be biblical and sincere. In so doing, we will be able "to exhort and to convince the gainsayers" (Titus 1:9). Wisdom is necessary to strike a balance between total abandonment for concern and empathy for the visitor.

Awkward Expressions

Not everyone was born with agility, grace, and rhythm. It is a good thing that the Lord does not require a graceful, physically balanced expression in praise, or else many people would be left out. God receives our praise when it is a real heart-felt expression, regardless of how awkward it may look. People look on the outward appearance, but God looks on the heart.

People will express themselves in praise within the framework of their personalities, within the boundaries of their abilities, and as a result of their influences. We cannot say that any particular expression is inherently sacred. Neither can we say that one method of praise is superior to another.

Even though God accepts our expressions of praise regardless of their awkwardness, that does not mean we should never seek to improve. Just as we should expand our praise vocabulary, so we should also endeavor to improve our expression of praise in other ways. Since our particular expression is not sacred, and in many instances it is a learned expression anyway, it is not sacrilege to make attempts to improve. In other words, there is nothing wrong with learning to clap with the rhythm of the music. If we are moved to demonstrate in some manner, there is nothing wrong with trying not to be clumsy. At the same time, we must not sacrifice spontaneity, freedom, or sincerity in order to look good to others.

Some have the misconception that they cannot demonstrate unless they are suddenly hit by a thunderbolt of the Holy Ghost. They feel that any demonstration without tremendous anointing is fleshly and not genuine worship. Sometimes these people will restrain themselves until they are about to explode under repressed emotion, for fear of "getting in the flesh." Then, when they can hold the emotion back no longer, they let go with a great shriek and a violent burst of uncontrolled contortions.

Although people who do this are sincere and are being blessed by the Holy Ghost, if they yielded to the Holy Ghost earlier and more naturally as their emotions began to build, perhaps a more graceful expression would result. There would be less possibility for accidents or misunderstanding by visitors. Perhaps the scream could be channeled into speaking in tongues or an anointed flow of verbal expressions of adoration to the Lord.

Paul admonished, "Quench not the Spirit" (I Thessalonians 5:19). Our praise should be free expression without tension or strain. We do not have to hold back on intensity or enthusiasm. At the same time we should remember, "the spirits of the prophets are subject to the prophets. For God is not the author of confusion, but of peace. . . . Let all things be done decently and in order" (I Corinthians 14:32-33, 40).

Destructiveness and Personal Injury

A few years ago, one church was sued because of injuries received during a worship service. An elderly lady stepped into the aisle just as a brother was running past. They collided in the aisle and the accident broke the lady's leg. She sued the church for $185,000 and won. The church suffered great embarrassment due to the publicity it received. This example illustrates the desirability for some regulation or direction for demonstrative worship.

It is uncomfortable to draw lines concerning physical methods of expression. Most churches need more proddings than restraints put on their praise. Nevertheless, drawing the line at destructiveness and injuries seems very appropriate. There is nothing unscriptural with trying to avoid such problems. If someone is going to run, it is not unscriptural to expect him to do so with his eyes open. Nor is it unscriptural to initiate some traffic control in a lively church service.

One pastor designated a worship area for men and another for women. Those who wanted to leave their pews in worship were instructed to go to these areas. He also requested those who wanted to run to always go in one direction around the sanctuary. He was criticized for putting rules on God and quenching the Spirit, but he continues to have a worshiping church and has avoided embarrassing situations without restricting the freedom of expression.

When injuries do occur, we cannot blame God. If we act carelessly by running with our eyes closed or veering too close to balcony railings, we must accept the responsibility for what happens. Just because we are doing something spiritual does not mean we are released from natural laws. We are still subject to the laws of gravity, friction, and brick walls.

Sometimes God does seem to protect the worshiper from disaster. Sometimes it appears that a worshiper is under such an anointing that his actions are involuntary and that God directs his steps to avoid harm. When I was a child, an elderly lady in our church was dancing during a tent revival and fell across a cinder block lying at the edge of the tent. Everyone thought surely she had been hurt. She rode home with us from church that night, and my mother asked her if the fall had hurt her. She assured us she was not hurt, and her explanation was amusing: "You know, the Lord finds the softest places for you to fall!"

God, at times, has mercy on our carelessness. Eutychus fell asleep during Paul's lengthy sermon at Troas and tumbled from the third loft. The Bible indicates that when the believers got to him he was dead. Paul embraced him and his life was restored (Acts 20:7-12). Nevertheless, we cannot always expect God to intervene miraculously to prevent harm, especially if our carelessness is deliberate.

We must seek the delicate balance between control and freedom, between order and spontaneity, between the planned and the impromptu. The worship service must continue to permit individual freedom of expression while at the same time be governed by God's divine order.

Worshiping God is a very sacred act. A mature understanding of God's majestic grandeur can only produce a feeling of awe and solemnity. As a result, our worship will have a dignity about it that shows reverence to our great God.

CHAPTER 11

Worship as a Way of Life

*P*eople do not choose whether or not they will worship; they only choose what they will worship. Humanity was created with an innate passion to worship something. "Worship is written upon the heart of man by the hand of God. It is not culturally induced, nor is it a learned experience. It is an inherent drive as real as food-seeking or self-preservation."[1]

Worship is a way of life. It is a prevailing influence that affects our morals, attitudes, lifestyle, and productiveness. What we worship forms the basis for our total philosophy of life, because what we worship controls our body, soul, and spirit. It is the thing to which we pay homage, submit, become obligated, and yield control.

People worship many false deities: false religions, sex, drugs, philosophy, money, power, communism, self, education, recreation, pleasure, and so on. The list could continue because humans are so diverse and life is so varied. These things, when worshiped, become obsessions and infiltrate every area of life.

For Christians, Jesus Christ is the pivotal point from whom life emanates and around whom life revolves. Jesus Christ is God incarnate; therefore, He rules as supreme, governing all attitudes and actions and providing moral principles by which Christians live.

Christian worship is not just a religious ritual in which people come together and do strange things in compliance to certain religious dogmas. Christians do not worship just at church, but their whole life becomes a lifelong pilgrimage of worship. The believer's body becomes a temple of worship, and communion with God is not limited strictly to geography, space, or schedule. Since God is omnipresent and worship is a spiritual endeavor, these things cannot determine worship.

The ultimate test for purity in Christian worship is the centrality of the Lord Jesus Christ. A love for the Lord will be the fulcrum of a well-balanced worship life.

A Thankful Attitude

True worship begins with a thankful attitude. The Christian gives thanks in all circumstances, good or bad. "Giving thanks always for all things unto God and the Father in the name of our Lord Jesus Christ" (Ephesians 5:20). "In every thing give thanks: for this is the will of God in Christ Jesus concerning you" (I Thessalonians 5:18).

Gratitude is not a natural virtue; it is a cultivated discipline. It is not based on the abundance of blessings, but it is based on a decision of the will. Helen Keller, who was blind and deaf, said, "I thank God for my handicaps, for through them I have found myself, my work and my God."[2] Her attitude is a good example of thankfulness.

206

Many spiritual and psychological problems are symptoms of an ungrateful attitude: self-pity, depression, worry, anger, frustration, and resentment. A thankful attitude is a key to overcoming such problems, for being thankful magnifies the positive and diminishes the negative. Thankfulness is a catalyst that electrifies life, making commitment a pleasure.

Being thankful should be a way of life for the Christian. He should become engulfed in a perpetual relationship with the Lord and not just consider Him at church. Prevailing thankfulness is foundational to the Christian life. Without it the Christian life is a series of cold choices, disciplines of the will, and performances of duty. Being thankful makes choices become divine guidance, disciplines become opportunities, and responsibilities become exciting challenges.

We can find ways to be thankful all through the day. By praising the Lord that we have health to rise out of bed in the morning, we will make getting up much easier. Giving thanks over our food is not just a religious habit, but it is an appropriate occasion to be thankful. The highways of our country are so dangerous these days that when we reach our destination safely it is a good time to give thanks. When people give us compliments, instead of taking all the glory, it is so befitting to give glory to the Lord. Meeting another Christian during the day is a good opportunity to say a hearty "Praise the Lord!" Having a close encounter with tragedy is a good time to give thanks. Seeing a disadvantaged person should motivate a thanksgiving for good health and blessings.

A young man once related to me the details of an automobile accident. His car skidded on wet pavement

207

and crashed into the oncoming traffic. The collision sent his car down a steep embankment. He climbed out of a demolished car without a scratch. He told me his first words were "Why me?" He did not see what danger he had escaped. His unthankful attitude caused him to see only his crashed car and the inconvenience the accident had caused.

Thankful people make good worshipers. The unthankful person will always find some distraction: he is tired, the temperature is not just right, the choir is not at its best, the preacher is boring, the people are unfriendly. On and on go the distractions for the unthankful.

Prayer

Prayer and worship are so intricately intertwined that they are almost impossible to separate. In fact, they are inseparable except when dissecting them for analytical purposes. In a broad sense, worship is prayer and prayer is worship. Their synergistic nature makes one powerless without the other.

Prayer is the most talked about of the Christian disciplines but the least practiced. Just the mention of the word makes many Christians feel guilty. Yet prayer and worship are two of the most powerful weapons we have to aid in our spiritual warfare.

There are many misconceptions about prayer. Many people think of prayer as something to do when in trouble and God is the only one who can help. To them, prayer is a monologue of request—just a time to catch God up on what's happening, to give God instructions, or to persuade God to do their bidding. This concept will greatly hamper the frequency and quality of prayer.

208

Prayer is communication with God, and it can be divided into three basic types.

1. *Supplication.* James 4:2 tells us simply, "Ye have not, because ye ask not." Petitioning the Lord is very scriptural. Asking is necessary before God will take action to supply the needs in our life. "Ask, and it shall be given you; seek, and ye shall find; knock, and it shall be opened unto you: for every one that asketh receiveth; and he that seeketh findeth; and to him that knocketh it shall be opened" (Matthew 7:7-8).

We have been given a host of promises in the Bible, and it is the will of God that they are fulfilled in our lives. Nevertheless, God respects our individual wills and does not act upon His promises if we do not seek them by faith in prayer. Even the saving of souls involves the prayers of God's people. God is the one who saves, and sinners must respond to Him in faith, but saints should intercede for the Lord to deal with people and draw them. "Pray ye therefore the Lord of the harvest, that he will send forth labourers into his harvest" (Matthew 9:38). (See also Isaiah 66:8.) Prayer is the key to revival!

2. *Communication.* Prayer is not a monologue of request but a dialogue of communication with God. This type of prayer includes telling God about circumstances and personal feelings; giving confessions and praises; making God our counselor, friend, and confidant. Surprisingly enough, God can talk back! In prayer we can receive divine guidance, comfort, and even rebuke from God.

At this level of prayer we become friends with God and establish a personal interaction. The Lord becomes more than just a guard of ethereal goodies whom we must cajole, beseech, and bargain with to get answers. We are not God's managers, dictating our wishes and coercing Him to comply. Neither are we like lawyers, pointing to promises and making demands on God. Through communicative prayer we can discern the mind of God in a matter and go beyond simply making petitions.

3. *Communion.* The deepest level of prayer is a level of intense expression. It generates feelings of intimacy with God, even to a point where words become unnecessary. Communion leads to worship in the fullest sense. It is void of request but permeated with unselfish expressions and feelings of gratitude to God. This level of prayer is characterized by a euphoric experience of overwhelming closeness to God. The Lord and the worshiper become as one. Although we may not always reach this level of prayer every time we pray, communion should be our ultimate goal. It is in communion that we worship completely. We forget ourselves and become lost in God's goodness.

It is noteworthy that the model prayer that Jesus gave begins with these words: "Our Father which art in heaven, Hallowed be thy name" (Matthew 6:9). Praise is a wonderful way to begin our prayer.

A few years ago I noticed that sometimes when I prayed I would become depressed, feeling worse than before I prayed. When I began to investigate, I found that this occurred during times of trouble in my life when my prayer deteriorated into just a worry session. I would agonize over my problem with very little faith. A few times I even remember leaving a prayer meeting with a headache. When I stopped fretting and started praising, things began to change for the better. Yes, praise and worship are wonderful faith builders.

It is also noteworthy that Jesus ended His prayer with praise: "For thine is the kingdom, and the power, and the glory, for ever. Amen" (Matthew 6:13). I once heard a preacher say that if he had ten minutes to pray, he would praise for eight minutes and pray for two. We cannot make a doctrine out of that statement, but neither is there anything wrong with it.

Judson Cornwall described the relationship between prayer and worship well:

> Prayer cannot successfully be separated from worship, for it prepares the soul for worship, expresses the spirit in worship, and interacts with God, which is worship.
>
> Worship without prayer is like daytime without light, a school without students, a choir without music, or an automobile without fuel.
>
> Prayer is entrance to our worship, the energy of our worship, the expression of our worship, and the enhancer of our worship.
>
> Prayer establishes worship, embraces worship, enlarges worship, and enlightens our worship.
>
> The praying saint cannot keep from worshiping; the prayerless saint cannot rise to worship.[3]

Discipleship

Many modern churches are infected with schizophrenic members. They are "Holy Joes" at church on Sunday and "Carnal Joes" during the week. They think worship is a modern mechanism with a convenient on-off switch. This dichotomous lifestyle indicates a lack of understanding or appreciation of the true nature of God.

211

For us to worship fully, Jesus must be not only our Savior but also our Lord. Living under the lordship of Jesus is the only way to become a true worshiper.

There is a close connection between the words *discipline* and *disciple*. To be a disciple of Jesus requires discipline. Training, exercise, development, subjection, correction, and self-control are involved in the process of discipleship. In an age of superficiality and instant gratification, discipline is an uncomfortable suggestion. People today are usually looking for shortcuts, instant results, and quick returns on their efforts. But this attitude is not conducive to discipleship and worship.

Discipline is not a negative chastisement or punishment of the flesh. "Neither should we think of Spiritual Discipline as some dull drudgery aimed at exterminating laughter from off the face of the earth. Joy is the keynote of all Disciplines. The purpose of the Disciplines is liberation from the stifling slavery to self-interest and fear. When one's inner spirit is set free from all that holds it down, that can hardly be described as dull drudgery."[4] Through the discipline of the flesh, as worship unto the Lord, we find true liberation in life.

The Bible commands us, "Worship the LORD in the beauty of holiness" (Psalm 29:2; 96:9; I Chronicles 16:29). Holiness is an essential factor in true worship. There is an old saying: "Words are pennies and deeds are dollars." What we say at church should be backed by a life of consecration and discipleship. Our whole life, our occupation, our relationships, our finances, our recreation, and our devotion should be a cathedral of praise and worship. Since we become the temple of the Holy Ghost at conversion, our whole life should be permeated with worship that results from our discipleship (I Corinthians 3:16). According to Jesus, loving God with all our being is the first commandment: "And thou shalt love the Lord thy God with all thy heart, and with all thy soul, and with all thy mind, and with all thy strength" (Mark 12:30).

Jesus told the woman at the well, "God is a Spirit: and they that worship him must worship him in spirit and in truth" (John 4:24). The word *spirit* is spelled with a small *s* in the major translations, which indicates that it refers to the human spirit. In other words, we are to worship with all the enthusiasm we can muster. To worship in truth means to back what we express verbally and emotionally by a life of discipleship in accordance with divine truth.

Obedience is the vital element that makes our discipline acceptable as worship. Discipline is not an end in itself. We do not inflict and endure certain tortures as acts of penitence. But obedience is an expression of true faith, and discipline is the natural result of our desire to please God. God rejected Saul's sacrifice because it was not done in obedience, and Samuel sternly rebuked him with these words: "Behold, to obey is better than sacrifice, and to hearken than the fat of rams" (I Samuel 15:22).

Sacrifice has no merit in itself. Many heathen religions outdo Christians in sacrifices and self-denial, but it is important to understand that these things are not measurements of truth. God rejected Israel's contaminated worship: "I hate, I despise your feast days, and I will not smell in your solemn assemblies. Though ye offer me burnt offerings and your meat offerings, I will not accept them: neither will I regard the peace offerings of your fat beasts. Take thou away from me the noise of thy songs; for I will

213

not hear the melody of thy viols" (Amos 5:21-23). "I have no pleasure in you, saith the LORD of hosts, neither will I accept an offering at your hand" (Malachi 1:10). The Pharisees made great sacrifices in prayers and fasting, yet they too were rejected because of hypocrisy (Matthew 23:23-28). The nation's sacrifices were to no avail because the people were unholy. God wants obedience more than sacrifice. Sacrifice should be a result of obedience, not a substitute for it, and the same is true of worship in general.

True worship motivates the worshiper to service. "If worship does not propel us into greater obedience, it has not been worship. Just as worship begins in holy expectancy it ends in holy obedience. Holy obedience saves worship from becoming an opiate, an escape from the pressing needs of modern life."[5] Worship at church and worship in daily discipleship are reciprocating; one accentuates the other.

A true worshiper understands that sacrifice is an important ingredient in worship. David sought to buy the threshing floor and oxen of Araunah the Jebusite to offer a sacrifice to God. Araunah offered to give David these things without charge, but David refused, saying, "I will surely buy it of thee at a price: neither will I offer burnt offerings unto the LORD my God of that which doth cost me nothing" (II Samuel 24:24).

We should offer holy lives as worship unto the Lord. Otherwise, personal, as well as collective, consecrations to the Lord can be easily misdirected into self-righteous motives. Our motivation for holiness must be more than conforming to certain rules, being accepted by the church, making points with God, or even improving our witness.

Our life of holiness should be done unto the Lord Jesus Christ, because we love Him and desire to please Him. Only then will He accept our lives and actions as true worship.

The Tabernacle teaches us much about worship today. The brazen altar was a place of sacrifice located just inside the Tabernacle courtyard. It sat immediately in front of the entrance, so it was the first object someone approached when coming through the gate. Hot coals were left burning on the altar day and night. This altar points to repentance, to daily consecration, and to the worship of discipleship.

The altar of incense was located inside the Tabernacle, immediately in front of the veil. It signifies communion in worship. It symbolizes the apex of the worship experience. Sweet spices were burned there, producing a fragrant aroma inside the Tabernacle as well as outside. Significantly, the fire used on the altar of incense was taken from the brazen altar. Any other fire was "strange fire." Similarly the worship we offer to God should originate in consecration, sacrifice, and discipleship. Worship that is not backed by a dedication is strange fire and unacceptable to the Lord.

For the worshiper to be qualified to worship he must be repentant. Jesus instructed, "Therefore if thou bring thy gift to the altar, and there rememberest that thy brother hath ought against thee; leave there thy gift before the altar, and go thy way; first be reconciled to thy brother, and then come and offer thy gift" (Matthew 5:23-24). Right relationships, attitudes, and purposes form a very important basis for real worship. Jesus was saying worship must be practiced not only at the altar but also in every area of life. At the altar we concentrate on worship and our communion with God reaches its climax. Nevertheless, consecration should be the axis around which all of worship revolves.

Worship and Work

I grew up thinking there were two types of Christians: the mediocre Christian worked in the secular work force and served God part time, and then there were sold-out Christians who worked full time for the Lord in the ministry. To really be used of God, I thought, a person had to be a preacher. I felt that those who had to work a secular job were just wasting time; it was just a necessary evil to provide money for the necessities of life.

Of course, this thinking is erroneous. Most workers will spend nearly one hundred thousand hours during their lifetimes doing secular work. Moses and David were shepherds, Amos was a picker of sycamore fruit, Nehemiah was a cupbearer to the king, Paul was a tentmaker, and Jesus was a carpenter. The secular work arena is one of the best places in the world for evangelism. It is also a great place to develop Christian character and to apply Christian principles.

Some feel that they must have a special calling before their work will be accepted as a worthwhile endeavor. Since preachers sometimes talk of a special calling on their lives, other Christians may feel they are doing nothing for God if they have not had a similar experience. Yet Daniel was imprisoned in Babylon, a victim of circumstances, and turned his predicament into a wonderful opportunity. There is no record of any special call; nevertheless, Daniel was productive, and God made him a great witness.

Work provides wonderful ways in which to worship God. Let us consider four ways that work can involve worship.

1. *Providing sustenance.* Solomon said, "Love not sleep, lest thou come to poverty; open thine eyes, and thou shalt be satisfied with bread" (Proverbs 20:13). Work provides increase: "He that gathereth by labour shall increase" (Proverbs 13:11). Being productive enables a person to provide for himself and avoid being dependent upon someone else. Thus, under normal circumstances, work is God's method of supplying our needs.

A worshiper will glorify the Lord in his work because he feels that it is worthwhile. His life will not be just an existence, but he will feel the invigorating satisfaction of his God-given productivity. The reward for his labor will stimulate a feeling of gratitude. Those who work will be made aware of their good health and will be motivated to praise. And the increase of the worshiping worker will enable him to give financially to the work of God.

Since the Fall, people have polluted everything they touch, including work. Many people worship their jobs and become "workaholics." Others are unthankful for the ability to work and refuse to work. Then there are those who think they are responsible for their financial blessings and refuse to give God the praise. But true worshipers know where their increase comes from and give praise to the Great Provider.

2. *Witnessing to the world.* The church is deliberately placed into the world to be a witness. Jesus made this clear in His prayer: "I pray not that thou shouldest take them out of the world, but that thou shouldest keep them from the evil" (John 17:15). We are to mingle with the

217

world and have a redemptive influence upon it. Our preserving influence is revealed in our designation as the "salt of the earth" (Matthew 5:13). The necessity of our visibility is indicated in the next verse: "Ye are the light of the world. A city that is set on an hill cannot be hid" (Matthew 5:14). We do not isolate ourselves into communal settings to be spiritual. This idea has been attempted many times and always results in failure. It is the will of God for us to mix with the people of the world so that they may observe our lifestyle, which should point them to Jesus.

Some of my greatest opportunities to witness came in the workplace. On one occasion, I was called into the supervisor's office and given a raise in pay. Two of my supervisors, who were both non-Christians, were very complimentary about my work habits. When both of them had finished their nice comments, I took the opportunity to tell them why I worked hard—I was a Christian, and I did what I did unto the Lord. Had I not been a good employee, this opportunity to witness would have never occurred. The best way to witness to the boss is to be the best employee he has. Then when the Christian has an occasion to witness the boss will listen.

When I was a manager, the employees would report to me when they were late or absent. They would have to explain their situation to me, and I would determine if they were excused. As a result, many times I became a counselor to troubled young men and was able to witness to them about the Lord. I also found many ways to implement Christian principles by being fair, showing kindness, being honest, and communicating with people in a godly way.

Even though our world is evil, we do not fulfill our Christian mission by becoming isolationists. As Paul said, "Be not overcome of evil, but overcome evil with good" (Romans 12:21). Jesus overcame the world, and He expects us to follow His example (John 16:33).

3. *Creative expression.* Jesus told a parable about a man who traveled to a far country and gave talents (money) to his servants. To one he gave five, to another he gave two, and to another he gave one. While the man was away, the servant with five doubled his talents. The servant with two doubled his also. But the servant with one hid his in the earth. Upon the master's return he rewarded the two faithful servants, but he stripped the slothful servant of his talent and cast him out. (See Matthew 25:14-30.)

This parable tells us, first of all, that all our blessings and abilities are gifts from God. Therefore, we should worship Him for this endowment and not claim personal glory. Second, God expects us to be good stewards of those gifts by putting them to use. By working in our field of labor we exercise our gifts and give glory to God. Third, God has given us what He wants us to have. In His sovereignty, He alone determines what we have. By accepting our role and fulfilling it with all our might, we acknowledge the sovereignty of God.

No one is without a gift. Since God created us in His image, we all have characteristics that are like Him. Moreover, God is still in the process of continually molding us after his fashion. When we use our God-given talents and abilities we become wise stewards of God's creative power. Our creative expression— whether it be building, managing, guarding, selling, or teaching—is all to be done to the glory of the Lord.

Good stewards maximize what they have, developing it to the fullest degree possible. A worker who produces poor work is not a good steward, and in turn, he is not a good worshiper. He is failing to give glory to the ultimate Creator. All labor, including physical labor, is honorable. Even though Paul was a great apostle, he still labored working with his hands as a tentmaker (I Corinthians 4:12).

4. *Personal fulfillment.* God created people with a basic need to have a function in life. People have a thirst for adventure and constantly seek for challenge. They must find interesting ways to fill up the time in their lives and produce some achievements as a result. Human dignity is found in work. The sluggard is an unhappy, depressed, and unfulfilled person because he misses all of these things. An unproductive person is not a good worshiper. He does not provide himself as a channel through which God can flow. His self-esteem will be low, causing him to be unthankful.

Probably all of us have dreamed of suddenly becoming excessively rich. We visualize what it would be like on a perpetual vacation with no responsibility, never having to work again. Sitting in the shade drinking lemonade may be a nice reprieve for a few days, but sooner or later it will become boring. We cannot remain in an occupational suspension for long. There is a driving need within all of us to find some positive purpose in life where our gifts can be put to use. God put this basic nature in us that we might become productive, and work fulfills God's plan for our lives.

Notes

[1]Judson Cornwall, *Elements of Worship* (South Plainfield, NJ: Bridge Publishing, 1985), p. 11.

[2]Merlin R. Carothers, *Power in Praise* (Escondido, CA: 1972).

[3]Judson Cornwall, p. 99.

[4]Richard J. Foster, *Celebration of Discipline* (New York: Harper and Row, 1978), p. 2.

[5]Ibid., p. 148.

Epilogue

Worship is not just a Pentecostal peculiarity, a charismatic idiosyncrasy, or a cultic exercise. It is not esoteric nonsense of a select group. It is a prevailing theme that runs the gamut of God's Word. Worship was practiced before the creation of humanity, and it will be a prominant activity throughout eternity to come. Worship is the recognition of ultimate reality; it is acknowledging the supremacy of God and the deficiencies of humanity. It is not abnormal to worship; in fact, not to worship is abnormal. Worship is the supreme purpose of humanity.

Throughout history, men and women who have touched God and whom God has touched have been people who knew how to enter the throne room of God and bow before Him, lifting up holy hands in adoration and acclamation. They were people who could encounter God personally and adore Him with phrases such as "Blessed be the Lord!" and "Hallelujah!"

Praise and worship should permeate every area of our lives. Our prayer should be saturated with praise. Our work and our exercise of talents should be offerings of praise. Our commitment to discipleship should be motivated by a sincere desire to glorify God's majesty. Even our recreation should be seasoned with adoration for the Lord. Every church service should be a celebration, with Jesus Christ as the celebrity.